Welcome Stress!

It can help you be your best

Welcome! Stress.

It can help you be your best

William D. Brown, Ph.D.

CompCare® publications

Brown, William D. (William David), 1936-
    Welcome Stress!

    Bibliography: p.
    1. Stress (Psychology) I. Title.
BF575.S75B76   1983   158'.1   83-20861
ISBN 0-89638-067-X (pbk.)

Inquiries, orders, and catalog requests should be addressed to
CompCare Publications
2415 Annapolis Lane
Minneapolis, Minnesota 55441
Call toll free 800/328-3330
(Minnesota residents 559-4800)

Jacket design by Susan Rinek

To Nett
on whose bright disposition
the sun
will never set

Contents

Stress Inventories

Introduction

Stress: much discussed, little understood; ever present, never absent; sometimes positive, occasionally negative; good and bad; desirable and undesirable; frequently sought out or energetically avoided. Paradoxical! That's stress—this and much more.

Forces within each of us cause one person to be hostile and combative, yet help another perform heroic feats far beyond what seem possible. While not all stress is desirable, we can honestly welcome stress when we're prepared to respond to it. Thus it is not stress itself but our response which will determine whether it is good or bad, negative or positive, desirable or undesirable.

Stress comes to all, but what creates *distress* (undesirable stress) for one results in *eustress* (desirable stress) for another. Boxers at the end of a fight are both stressed: the loser most likely distressed, while the winner is ecstatically eustressed. The homeowner who is burglarized is distressed; the thieves are presumably eustressed.

From our first waking moment to the final reflection passing across the mental thought-screen just before we drift off to sleep, stress is a constant companion. Stress continues even in our sleep, though with the exception of dreams which become conscious, we remain oblivious to it. Stress is involved in all human interactions, both in the home and on the job. It affects every living organism, even animals.

As I write this introduction, I have just returned from an early summer morning's ride on our quarter horse, Scooter, through rolling hills here in the Virginia countryside. Such an early excursion before turning to more substantive affairs is refreshing and relaxing—for the rider. However, as our gelding is put through the paces of a morning workout, trotted through fields, galloped over open pasture, and encouraged to jump creeks, the thought occurs that his level of distress may be equal to my level of eustress. As I relax in the saddle, a whippoorwill is routed from her nest in tall, thick grasses. Occasionally a mother rabbit is scared from her well-hidden hutch by the thundering hooves breaking the serenity of quiet fields. The ride, creating stress for rider and mount, results in eustress for the former but obviously causes varying degrees of distress for both Scooter and the creatures who have been disturbed.

The purpose of this book is to help each of us better understand stress as a phenomenon, and furthermore, to welcome and seize the opportunities stress presents to us each day. Part One is an overview of stress as it affects the total or whole person. This holistic approach, emphasizing our physiological, sociological, psychological, and spiritual needs, is the only way to understand the multiple ramifications of stress. Applying the stress inventories from this section to your own life will help you assess how well you cope with stress.

Part Two addresses specific causes of stress in the home and on the job. Use this section to improve your own mechanisms to cope with the myriad of stresses encountered as a result of interacting closely with others. By taking these inventories and scoring yourself, you will be able to determine if you are (1) experiencing too much stress, and/or (2) handling adequately the stress you feel.

Part Three discusses emotionally efficient ways to cope with stress. Learning to welcome stress can help you become the kind of person you would like to be, with far-reaching personal and vocational effects.

Greater happiness awaits you if you will honestly assess yourself, determining how you have responded to stress during the past and how you can prepare to handle it better in the future.

Welcome Stress! It Can Help You Be Your Best is an especially fitting book for all Americans, individually and collectively. Remember that the last four letters in the word "American," are *"I can."* As a nation of doers, we have frequently felt we have a monopoly on the "can do" spirit, but recent years have shown that other nations are equally adept at producing quality goods competitive with those manufactured here. While such recognition has caused distress for many in both management and labor, it is the contention here that these challenges from abroad should be welcomed, stirring us out of a growing work apathy that has plagued our productivity since the close of World War II. Meeting these challenges can provide a kind of eustress which can prove to be the turning point in helping us regain the pride in products stamped "Made in America." We're also reminded that in any field of endeavor we have but one real source of competition: *ourselves!*

Dizzy Dean once observed, "It ain't braggin' if you can do it." We Americans have been happier and more productive in the past. We can be so again, which is the jumping-off place for this book inviting you to take Virgil's wisdom to heart in beginning a journey which will prove most beneficial when recalling his simple yet eloquent phrase, "They can who think they can." I think you can be happier, more productive and contented by welcoming stress and making it work *for* you.

With proper approaches and attitudes, stress need seldom become distress, for as Napoleon Hill reminds us in *Think and Grow Rich,* "Whatever the mind of man can conceive and believe, it can achieve." If thoughts always precede action, let's begin with a self-improvement program learning to *Welcome Stress! It Can Help You Be Your Best!*

William D. Brown
Shadyside

Summer, 1983

Part One

Becoming a Whole Person

·1·

Position Yourself to Welcome Stress

Harry left the corporation boardroom early in the day with a feeling of exhilaration he hadn't experienced in years. All those fifteen-hour days, late evenings at work, missed weekends and holiday family outings due to the rigorous demands of his job have finally paid off handsomely.

Though he is the youngest member of the board, Harry was elected a vice-president of the firm just this morning, assuring him of a continued board seat and, more importantly, a place on the executive committee which sets company policy. Now he will have a generous expense account, a corner office in the company's skyscraper office building, and — perhaps most important of all — the prestigious plum of having one of the firm's most competent secretaries assigned solely to him.

He heads back to his office with pounding heart, spirits lifted, and a feeling of rejuvenation, though he has had little sleep this past week. Never has he been quite so happy! The thought crosses his mind that this must be the kind of "natural high" some talk about. Just think, he pleasantly muses: this high has resulted solely from his efforts and hard work over the last five years since joining the firm. Today is one of those unusual, mountain-top experiences that rarely come into any life. He savors it for a long time, once back in his office.

That same morning across town, another of the firm's employees, Walt, lies very still in bed, aware that this will be one of the most difficult days of his life. Last night he slept alone again, only now for the first time in thirty-three years, he knew this would forever after be his lot, because his wife—the confidante, helpmate, and love of his life—died yesterday. Today he would have to meet with the funeral director to make plans for putting to rest the best friend he ever had.

Lying there, Walt's mind races back over the years. He recalls their shared joy when she first became pregnant and then the pride they had taken in each child's accomplishments. Memories of special moments of closeness between the pair flash across his mind as if projected from a movie reel feeding too quickly through the camera. Scenes from yesteryears seem so vivid and clear: their first date, the marriage ceremony in the small church packed with friends and family members, loved ones also now departed who gave so much of themselves to the young couple, trying times when money was tight, the day they first learned of her serious illness, and up through last week, when prior to her coma they had continued sharing a bond neither could adequately describe or ever hope to duplicate.

Walt's heart pounds as he contemplates getting out of bed. If only his mind would stop racing and the empty feeling in the pit of his stomach would go away, he could cope with the day's pressures. Already he was nervous and tense, perspiring even though the house was quite comfortable with the steady background humming as the air-conditioning unit whined along. Today would be hard, he knew. If only he could escape having any part of it, but such could not be.

In a third home, Barb, forty-two and married for twenty years, saw her husband off to work at his job with this same corporation. The children just left for school and Barb pauses to contemplate her noon engagement. There is just enough time left to fix her hair, do her nails, and luxuriate in a warm bath before meeting one of her husband's business associates for lunch. This will be the third time he has taken her to lunch at an expensive restaurant, showering her with attention which has grown increasingly flirtatious in ways she could scarcely remember even from early days of courtship.

She recognizes her infatuation in this relationship is shifting from enjoyment of a close friendship to increasing feelings of greater intimacy. Mixed feelings arise in her, for while morally she is opposed to developing this relationship further, she feels life is slipping away and desperately wants to capture forever the feeling that coursed through her body the two previous times when she was out with this man. Yet, she knows it is wrong, and a momentary shiver of guilt runs through her body as she reflects on her marriage, family, and all that's inevitably at stake.

She notices her heart racing, her palms sweaty, and feels extremely anxious, a kind of general anxiety, for she relates this momentary feeling of panic to nothing specific. "After all," she tells herself, "this really is innocent, regardless of what others might think." In any event, now she must hurry and, she muses, recalling an episode from a literature course almost a quarter of a century ago, Margaret Mitchell had the right idea when she wrote the famous line in her epic novel, *Gone with the Wind:* "Tomorrow is another day." "Yes," Barb agrees, "tomorrow *is* another day." Hurriedly she sets off to begin preparations which always make her feel as she had on those first dates with her mate over two decades ago.

Common Factors

What are common factors in these three lives? Aside from Harry, Walt, and Barb's husband employed by the same corporation, all are involved in crises ultimately affecting their respective families and without exception, experiencing the inner turmoil arising from that condition called change, described by Heraclitus in 500 B.C. when he observed that nothing in life is permanent except change. In addition to intense personal change, each finally share one other major factor: *stress.*

The sweaty palms, racing minds, heavy and joyous hearts, specific and general anxiety, exhilaration over a feat finally accomplished, as well as the dread of the day ahead—all are signs indicating stress. These signs or symptoms are the body's response to change. Never mind that Harry views his job change via promotion as desirable, that Walt feels the change brought about by the death of his mate as totally undesirable, or that Barb sees her emotional response as a mixture: she is torn between stopping and continuing her extramarital involvement. In each instance, the body responded similarly, for stress as a process doesn't discriminate between desirable or undesirable events.

Dr. Hans Selye, the endocrinologist who pioneered work in the area of stress, defines stress as "the nonspecific response of the body to any demand made upon it." As noted, stress cannot be classified as either good or bad. Rather, in the sense that the body responds to the pressure of stress, the reaction is similar for individuals recently fired or their counterparts who have just been promoted. The salesman who has finally made that long-sought sale, accounting for most of his efforts these past few months, experiences similar body responses resulting from stress as does another salesman and close friend, who today learned that his equally long-courted prospect placed that major order with a competitor. In each case, the body responds in a nonspecific manner resulting in both physical and emotional changes.

The body begins to respond to stress in that part of the brain known as the hypothalamus, which is the part controlling growth, sex, and reproduction abilities. It is also the seat of fear, rage, and intense pleasure. Now we begin to understand how stress levels can lead to heights of pleasure or to depths of despair.

In spite of its dual nature, stress is to be welcomed, for without it, little would be accomplished. For instance, if you hadn't experienced certain levels of stress early in life, you would never have acquired the ability to read. You would not now be embarking on a venture to use stress more constructively in your life had you not been motivated via some level of stress to learn to read.

Another example of stress as a positive motivator is simply getting up in the morning. Many people would find it easier to stay in bed than to arise and start a new day. Certainly this will be confirmed by those who do not consider themselves "morning" people. Yet, stress mounts if we remain in bed too long, for few enjoy getting the day off to a bad start by being late.

Stress, then, can be viewed as a condition causing us to behave in desirable ways. Our past accomplishments can be traced to those times when we felt stressed enough to tackle necessary tasks getting on with our work. In this sense stress is good, helping us to live up to the best that is within us.

Two Types of Stress

Eustress (from the Greek root *eu* meaning "good") is one type of stress. Eustress is the conversion of stress within you when you choose the harder right over the easier wrong, when you live up to what you want to be rather than down to what you might become.

Stress converted to positive energy is stress helping you be your best. It is what has enabled you to accomplish much in the past, reach those high goals you set for yourself, and contributed to your reputation as a person to be counted upon, even when you didn't feel like coming through. Eustress is stress being converted and used positively and responsibly. This is a desirable outcome of stress.

The opposite of eustress is *distress* (coming from the Latin root *dis* meaning "bad"). Stress converts to distress when you tell the first lie, when you cheat, or when you wrestle with the knowledge of having done something wrong or illegal, even though other people may never know.

Stress which becomes distress in your life is stress serving you at your worst. This occurs when you fail to be the person you could be or dwell on thoughts which you know will only cause you difficulty later. It's distress when you allow yourself to get down, choosing to be negative. Negative thinking never seems to need substantiating as does the positive, so it is much easier to be pessimistic than optimistic.

Each of these two types of stress, eustress and distress, is dependent on conditions present. In competition the winner's stress usually converts to eustress; for the loser, stress becomes distress. No one likes to lose, so our interest focuses on ways to turn initial distress into eustress. Consider the sales manager who is gifted at inspiring and leading people, but who dreads to stand up and address his sales people at weekly sales meetings. He might silently wish he were not so nervous and tense. Yet, would he perform as well were he relaxed at the outset and devoid of all stress?

Such a sales manager begins by being concerned with his performance, so initially he feels distressed. After the meeting, however, recognizing that he performed well because his salespeople congratulate him for his inspirational presentation, this same internal stress now becomes eustress. Some of you might reply, "Yes, but this doesn't apply to me." However, in reality, all of us are salespeople—selling a product, an idea, a philosophy, or trying to convince others to do things our way.

Conversely, all of us are customers in one way or another several times daily. For example, we feel eustress when we proudly accept delivery of the much-desired new car ordered weeks earlier. In contrast, time spent in waiting in long lines or dealing with slow or surly salespeople is usually experienced as distress.

As family members, we are continually interacting with loved ones. Initial frustrations with them can be turned into contentment in time as we better understand their views, even if we don't agree. Hence, the distress of parent with child, child with parent, spouse with spouse, or relative with relative, can ultimately become eustress if for no other reason than the recognition we have done all in our power to go the second mile in understanding why others feel as they do.

Stress Is Desirable

There is a Chinese proverb that states, "When God is angry with man, He answers his prayers." Sometimes those things we want most are later recognized as possibly the worst choices we could have made. Once again, in time, initial

7

distress becomes eustress as we realize that the best choice was made in spite of earlier desires. Robert Preston, star of stage and screen, once commented, "It seems to me that every disappointment I've ever had has been followed by the thing I should have done in the first place."

Someone once described the absence of stress as a condition known as rigor—followed closely by mortis! So long as there is a life in the body, from the first wail of the infant to the last gasp at the end of life, there will be stress.

Overload or Underload

"Individuals can become either overloaded or underloaded with stress," wrote Rosalind Forbes in *Corporate Stress.* To be overloaded with stress involves an awareness of intense pressure, a sense of having too much to do in too little time, and feeling harried and frustrated as a result. Conversely, stress underload occurs when there is too little pressure. This affects individuals at work who feel overqualified for their jobs. Workers who believe they have reached impassable plateaus in their careers, who have gone as far as they can, or recognize no ways open for further advancement, may be experiencing stress underload, a form of distress.

Symptoms of stress underload on the job range from a high rate of absenteeism ("executive hooky"), work avoided whenever possible or increased drinking problems, to more cases of marital infidelity. This "acting out" occurs not because the person is bad, but rather because stress is converted to distress as a result of frustration, harassment, and/or poor earlier choices. This kind of stress is handled constructively when one recognizes that stress underload is as dangerous as stress overload and takes appropriate action to correct the situation.

Obviously, the more of our stress we can convert to eustress, the better off we are. Naturally, though, it is impossible to convert *all* stress to eustress. The loss of a loved one, a forced retirement, the loss of a job, or a child who has failed to do something reasonably constructive with his life—all are events which most likely result in stress that is converted to distress, at least temporarily.

Holistic Approach

We will never be able to cope effectively with stress until we recognize the need to become whole persons. The self cannot be segmented into competing parts; rather, it must be viewed as a whole. Emotions can no more be separated from our physical beings than desire from love.

To become whole persons, we must make certain our needs are met in each of four areas:

> physiological
> sociological
> psychological
> spiritual

Healthiest individuals are those who live balanced lives with their needs sufficiently met in these four areas. These needs will be considered at length in the remainder of this section.

Stress Inventory I
Signs of Stress

Do you recognize signs of stress when they occur? Awareness of these signs can help you recognize stress early, channeling it into eustress rather than distress.

Remember: *you are not trying to eliminate stress but to direct it so that most of your stress will not lead to distress.*

Carefully read the following behaviors and physical reactions, putting a "1" in front of the ones which *nearly always* accompany stress for you. Then read the list again, rating with a "2" those which *sometimes* occur with your stress. Finally, record a "3" beside those which happen *infrequently.*

_____	Depression	_____	Rapid pulse rate
_____	Withdrawal	_____	Increased
_____	Hyperactivity		perspiration
_____	Compulsiveness	_____	Pounding heart
_____	Muscle tension	_____	Tightened stomach
_____	Shortness of breath	_____	Appetite loss
_____	Gritting teeth	_____	Overeating
_____	Biting lips	_____	Sleeping more
_____	Disrupted sleep		frequently or longer
	patterns		than usual
_____	Excessive emotional	_____	Clenching jaw
	display	_____	Racing thoughts

Study your own ratings. Often just recognizing how you react in certain situations will give you the opportunity to improve or even eliminate the negative effects of stress. Pay particular attention to those you've rated a "1." Are there ways you can rechannel your energy, avoiding the most troublesome symptoms of stress?

·2·

The Body Saved Will Be Your Own

A classic study in understanding the forces behind man's drives is Maslow's hierarchy of needs (see figure 1). This needs hierarchy ascends from the most basic needs at the base of the pyramid to a higher order of needs at its peak.

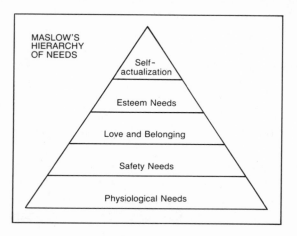

Figure 1. Maslow's needs hierarchy from A.H. Maslow, *Motivation and Personality,* New York: Harper, 1954.

Individuals are obviously little interested in self-fulfillment until they first feel loved. Love in turn is not a primary need until people feel safe and secure, which remains unimportant so long as their bodies are undernourished. Therefore, it is of utmost importance that our bodies be treated well before higher need levels can be met.

Need for Food

Oscar Wilde once noted that nothing succeeds like excess.* Certainly he didn't have the average American's eating habits in mind, for our preoccupation and overindulgence with food is an excess that has been anything but successful. In fact, being several pounds overweight is a national malaise affecting most Americans. Many people eat not because they are hungry but rather to satisfy emotional needs, with these patterns sometimes traceable to early childhood. Reared in a home where they were fed whenever upset, children learned to associate eating with stress. Often this pattern is carried into adulthood, so that overeating has little to do with nourishment needs, but rather compensates for unmet emotional needs.

Furthermore, from corporate executives to day laborers, workers frequently eat poorly. Missed meals are often followed by catch-up eating. Crash food intake may lead to indigestion or heartburn, but entirely too many overindulgers take a break just long enough for the symptoms to subside before they binge again.

Intelligent nutrition requires that we neither over- nor under-eat, that we recognize the body's need for three regular meals each day of foods representing the four basic food groups—meat, poultry and fish; cereal and bread; fruits and

---

*Wilde was paraphrasing the French proverb, "Nothing succeeds like success."

vegetables; and dairy products. Also, starches, fats, and "junk food" should be avoided whenever possible.

Several organizations have been founded with the sole purpose of helping the overweight restructure and control their eating habits. Though the programs have not been equally successful, adherents to the various plans have generally benefited from an organized approach to losing weight and especially by support received from other members in the group.

Another effective way to lose weight is to convert the distress of being overweight to the eustress of observing a weight reduction when you step on the bathroom scales. The secret is finding and staying with an approach that will motivate you toward your desired goal.

A good idea for males who want to lose weight is to find a picture of a male physique they would like to emulate. Then attach the picture to the inside of the medicine cabinet door so they will see it each morning when shaving. This silent reminder of what they want to look like will register mentally at both conscious and subconscious levels throughout the day, reinforcing their goals of serious weight reduction.

Females can do the same thing, placing a picture of a woman whose figure they admire on a door or mirror where it will be seen at least twice a day. This approach will do wonders to motivate them subliminally, as many women could readily attest.

A word of caution, particularly for the young female: any unusual weight loss or drastic change in appetite should be discussed with a physician *immediately.* Obviously there can be too much of any good thing, including weight loss. When loss of weight becomes an obsession, it can signal the onset of a serious disease called anorexia nervosa, often described as a "young woman's disease," generally affecting females from upper-and middle-class backgrounds. It involves loss of appetite, believed to stem from psychological rather than physiological causes. This psycho-physiological disease seizes control of eating habits. Symptoms include excessive weight loss which may result in cessation of menstruation, spells of compulsive eating frequently followed by induced vomiting or days of starvation, and a distorted body image. Other symptoms include being obsessed with food, even dreaming about it, and/or preparing elaborate dinners but refusing to eat them. Also, the victim fails to perceive that her physical condition has seriously deteriorated.

Dr. Hilde Bruch, professor of psychiatry at Baylor College of Medicine in Houston and an authority on anorexia nervosa, has said, "Starvation is merely a symptom and not the real problem. The main thing I've learned is that the worry about being skinny or fat is not the real problem. The real illness has to do with how you feel about yourself." A fundamental problem is the fear in the young woman that she cannot live up to what is expected of her. What follows is the anorexic's ability to prove she has control, that indeed she can accomplish something no one else can. Other psychotherapists speculate that the disease represents a rejection of adulthood, with a refusal to accept sexual maturity.

Many people believe that normal, healthy young girls are trapped into a pattern leading to anorexia nervosa by dieting, but usually this is not the case. There is nearly always an underlying emotional cause precipitating the disease. Detected early, anorexia can be treated on an outpatient basis.

Like stress, food is neither good nor bad—the question is how it is used or abused. Too much or too little food will create stress for the body which will most likely be converted to distress and, therefore, either extreme should be scrupulously avoided.

Need for Drink

It is said that man can live for seven days without water, for fourteen days without food, and for a lifetime without an original thought! Actually, humans can survive for varying periods without food, dependent on their condition at the outset of the ordeal. However, no one can exist long without water. The body needs ample water or other liquid refreshment each day in order to survive. For most individuals the problem doesn't involve the quantity but the *kinds* of liquid.

Not long ago our quarter horse mare gave birth to a colt. Our teenage daughter named him "Rocky." Rocky is an exceptionally large colt whose emerging permanent coat hints that he will be buckskin with a raven-black mane, tail, and leggings. Broad through the chest, he appears to be a superb quarter horse stud, with a pedigree which would be admired by anyone familiar with this breed. We take good care of Rocky, seeing that he is adequately fed and watered each day. At night we make certain he is locked in the barn so he won't hurt himself on any of the pasture fencing. We have had the veterinarian out several times to examine Rocky, giving him shots, and once to stitch a tear in the skin on his hock. We reason he warrants all this care because, after all, we expect to sell him for a handsome sum.

It occurred to me at feeding time one day that we take far better care of some of our less valuable possessions than those of much greater value. For instance, we wouldn't think of keeping Rocky up until all hours of the night, nor would we dream of failing to feed or water him. Other than milk from his mother, his feed is controlled: no junk food is fed our colt, and we would certainly never give him access to liquids we thought might harm him.

However, people frequently stay up all night pursuing activities which at least occasionally do them far more harm than good. Meals are skipped if something more interesting comes along, with non-nutritional foods consumed in record amounts. Yet, these same people would profess that humans are far more valuable than other forms of animal life.

Anything injurious to health is endangering one of our most valuable assets — our bodies! This becomes a critical issue considering the abuse of alcohol in our society.

The number of alcoholics in America is unknown, but some authorities believe it equals the population of the state of Texas! Others believe this is a conservative figure, with the real number approximating twenty-five to thirty million! The alcoholic is one who cannot control his or her drinking, even when it damages health, job, family, and/or mind.

Typical warning signs of this disease include frequent use of alcohol to cope with daily stresses, with the problem drinker consuming increasingly larger amounts. The self-image deteriorates, with fears and anxieties increasing as the alcoholic's disease progresses. Responsibilities may be ignored, including those on the job or in the family setting. Arguments over drinking include accusations and denials about drinking habits, followed by promises to drink less in the future. Blackouts may occur with increased frequency, with the drinker unable to recall what happened while intoxicated.

Though the following questions, presented below as Stress Inventory II, are hardly foolproof, answering them "Yes" or "No" should be helpful in determining whether you have a problem with alcohol. The questions can be applied to a loved one, should you suspect alcoholism. One or more "Yes" answers indicates a possible drinking problem. It may also indicate a need to seek professional help, i.e., preferably counseling, treatment, and/or participation in the (AA) Alcoholics Anonymous program.

Stress Inventory II
Alcohol-Related Problem?*

Answer each of the following questions Yes or No.

———	1.	A drink is nearly always needed "the morning after."
———	2.	Time is lost from work or school because of drinking.
———	3.	He/She drinks alone or tries to hide the drinking.
———	4.	Loss of memory or loss of control occurs while or after drinking.
———	5.	He/She seems irritable, defensive, jealous, moody, or is easily angered following drinking.
———	6.	Drinking is denied or minimized. Criticism or complaints upset the drinker.
———	7.	Physical complaints, including inefficiency, low energy, weight loss, sleeplessness, or accidents are related to drinking.
———	8.	Guilt feelings or depression follow drinking bouts.
———	9.	Friends and social activities are avoided because of drinking.
———	10.	Family and/or friends are embarrassed, harmed, or worried about drinking behavior.

*Adapted from *Alcoholic in the Family?*, American Association of Marriage and Family Therapists, Claremont, California, 1977, p. 5.

Family members of problem drinkers need not sit idly by, watching alcoholism take its inevitable toll. Once it was believed there was little others could do to help the problem drinker. Now, procedures are known and available to help the problem drinker's family cope with this illness for their own benefit, as well as the problem drinker's.

There are numerous life events which propel a person toward alcoholism, including a need to escape pressures or avoid rather than face problems. Drinking may be sought as an aid in dealing with loneliness, especially following the death of a loved one. However, drinking is but a temporary fantasy creating the illusion of a better situation. This cruel hoax becomes clear following a drinking bout, which causes the problem drinker to turn to alcohol once again in an attempt to ease resulting emotional pain. This cycle must be broken if the alcoholic is to have any hope of sobriety.

Family members and significant others can help the problem drinker in the following ways:

1. *Insist that he/she face the truth.* The sooner this is done the better. Avoid attempts to keep the drinking a secret from outsiders or other family members. Even very young children will quickly sense the nature of the problem.

2. *Learn the facts about alcoholism.* In large cities the National Council on Alcoholism sponsors alcohol information centers. Al-Anon offers help to family members of problem drinkers, including a special program, Alateen, which provides assistance for youth from ages twelve to twenty. Alcoholics Anonymous (AA) chapters are located nationwide. This self-help organization of recovering alcoholics provides a plan for recovery known as the Twelve Steps, a support group, and free regularly scheduled meetings.

3. *Strive to build a healthy home atmosphere.* Do not forego pursuing outside interests and friendships because of

the problem drinker in your family. Isolation will but lead to further unhappiness, helping no one.

4. *Talk over the problem with some responsible person outside your home.* This may include your family clergyman, physician, psychologist, or counselor. These professionals frequently deal with those who are caught up in alcohol-related problems and will be helpful in assisting you to think through the best ways to deal with the situation.

5. *Be patient and compassionate with the problem drinker.* As a disease, alcoholism doesn't develop overnight, nor will it be arrested immediately. Let your problem drinker know you will love and respect him or her as a person, though you don't approve of the drinking.

6. *Understand your own emotions and be fair to yourself.* Depression, anger, and self-pity in the alcoholic's family members are common reactions. Feelings cannot be denied, but they can be dealt with and resolved.

Another typical feeling is guilt. However, acting on this feeling will not help, but may hinder the alcoholic's progress. Often the problem drinker attempts to blame others for the problem. Remember that you are not the cause of another's alcoholism any more than you can cause another's suicide. Assuming the blame for the drinking will help no one, least of all the alcoholic.

Finally, even though some believe that certain alcoholics may find that they can once again drink socially, thousands have found that, even after years of abstinence, the desire for alcohol is as intense as ever. *No alcoholic can afford the risk of discovering that he or she is but another one of the thousands who mistakenly thought it was possible to drink again.*

Need for Sex

Of all our physiological needs, sex probably receives more attention than any other. It is much discussed but seldom adequately understood. The assumption underlying much of the writing on this subject is that those who can perform adequately understand the nature and consequences of the sex drive. Nothing could be further from the truth! For instance, examine some rudimentary facts about sex and youth. The statistics boggle the mind, for never has a generation been so well-informed. Shouldn't this consequently change their behavior?

Before responding, consider the following:

—   Teenagers bear nearly one in five babies born in the United States;

—   Forty percent of these births are out of wedlock, accounting for one-half of the total out-of-wedlock births in the country;

—   One in six teenage females who has premarital intercourse will become pregnant;

—   Only three out of ten sexually active teenage females use contraception consistently;

—   Among those not using contraceptive devices, seven in ten think they cannot become pregnant; and

—   Those aged fifteen to nineteen are three times more likely to contract gonorrhea than those over age twenty, with their risk of syphilis 60 percent greater.[1]

Yet, shrill voices continue to clamor for the cessation of sex education, as if not talking about the subject will give rise to sexual abstinence! No one ever erred because of too much knowledge, though everyone is aware of poor judgments arising in a vacuum of ignorance. In some major American cities the illegitimate birth rate already exceeds the legitimate birth rate. This problem deserves the attention of all responsible persons, as its long-range effects for society are fearsome.

An interest in sex is normal for males and females from late puberty to the grave. In fact, most people recognize that it is impossible to separate their sexuality from the rest of their beings. Once it was believed that sexual interest ceased beyond seventy years old, but scientists now recognize that a healthy interest in sex is normal as long as there is life.

Sex between a husband and wife fulfills not only the couple's physical needs, but since the physical cannot be separated from psychological or emotional needs, sexual gratification has ramifications far beyond the obvious. When two partners sufficiently meet each others needs a sense of trust is generated which reinforces the self-esteem of each person.

Hopefully, the last gasps have been heard from those who seriously proposed what they describe as the virtues of a sexual double standard, in which the male is free to be sexually involved with other females while the female is to remain monogamous. Marriages will inevitably benefit when there is a single sexual standard, where sex is not separated from love but rather recognized as an important contributing factor to the overall relationship.

In today's society the extramarital involvements of women are increasing, and perhaps this is a logical extension of "equal rights." But while agreeing that the same standard should hold for both sexes, do we need to settle for the worse of the two standards as a replacement for the old double standard? Why not choose the better of the two, applicable to *both* husbands and wives?

Sexual relations outside marriage severely strain the primary relationship. Feelings such as guilt and insecurity create emotional distance between spouses. On the other hand, feelings of trust and acceptance create an openness which makes the most intimate, satisfying marriage. This is what "open marriage" means at its best.

All our basic physiological needs should be taken more seriously, but this is particularly true for our sexual needs. Interestingly, Thoreau observed this over a hundred years ago when he wrote, "I lose my respect for the man who can make the mystery of sex the subject of a course jest, yet, when you speak earnestly and seriously on the subject, is silent."

Stress Inventory III
Building Relationships

1. List those qualities you prize most highly in a relationship with the significant person in your life, i.e., wife, husband, friend, etc.

   _____   _____
   _____   _____
   _____   _____
   _____   _____
   _____   _____

2. Go back and place a number before each quality you listed, putting each in rank order with "1" the most highly prized quality and "10" the least important.

3. Read the list a second time. Recall as best you can how you felt at the outset of your relationship with this person. Now rank these items as they applied at that time.

4. How do you account for the difference?

5. Dr. Clark Vincent, formerly of the Bowman Gray Medical School faculty once observed, "Men and women approach each other from opposite ends of the spectrum: at least in dating relationships, men give love in order to obtain sex, while women give sex in order to obtain love." Do you agree or disagree with this statement? Why or why not?

6. Would you agree or disagree when applying the statement to marriage?

Need for Exercise

Heart attack is the number one cause of death in America. For overweight people with high levels of fat and high cholesterol counts, high blood pressure, and a heavy cigarette habit, the risk of heart attack is five times greater than average.[2] Further, it is important to note that the two most significant factors in preventing heart attack are diet and exercise.

Exercise prolongs life, reduces the level of cholesterol in the blood, makes the heart a more efficient pump, and increases the number and size of blood vessels. Exercise also increases the amount of oxygen the body can use, helps reduce blood clots, and assists in controlling weight. Just as dieting is not the sole answer to weight control, neither is exercise. Of course, no weight program should be undertaken without first consulting your physician.

Many comparison research studies have been conducted in attempts to measure the importance of exercise as it relates to sickness and death. One of the more ambitious studies undertaken in this regard was that of researchers at the Harvard School of Public Health in conjunction with those at Trinity School of Medicine in Dublin, Ireland.[3] This study compared the health over a ten-year period of 600 Irish-born men who had come to Boston with the health of their brothers who had remained in Ireland. The ages for these brothers differed by no more than five years.

After living here for ten years, the brothers who had come to America had approximately twice the number of deaths due to heart disease. For once the blame could not be placed on the American diet, for the brothers who remained in Ireland ate an average of 500 calories more per day than did their American counterparts, and these calories included far more butter and eggs, foods which are known for raising blood cholesterol levels. However, average blood cholesterol levels for those remaining in Ireland was 13 percent lower than the level for those who had come to America. Further, despite a higher intake of calories, the brothers in Ireland weighed 8 to 10 percent less than American siblings. Even more astounding, these brothers were lean and muscular in contrast to those who had moved to America.

The chief difference between those brothers who stayed in Ireland and those who came to America was that the former group worked harder physically in a society where there were fewer conveniences to help ease the workload. For example, when they left home, they traveled mostly on foot or by bicycle. This was in marked contrast to the brothers who had come to America and had grown accustomed to all types of labor-saving devices. The results were obviously disastrous!

Other studies focusing on different populations have reported similar findings. More postal clerks were found to suffer heart attacks than mailmen who walked their daily rounds. Railroad clerks had a heart-attack death rate twice that of switchmen and maintenance workers, both latter groups being more physically active in their work. The singular, outstanding message from all this research is that exercise reduces a person's chances of heart attack.

Increasingly, Americans are taking more seriously the need for adequate exercise, but there is much room for improvement if we are seriously going to attack our national malaise of overweight and premature death rate due to improper physical conditioning. The benefits from getting—and staying—in peak condition are enormous for everyone. Future dividends are far greater for those who act now on this vital need for exercise.

Need for Rest

Dividing the twenty-four hours in a day by three makes available eight hours for work, eight for refreshment and relaxation, and eight for rest and sleep. The problem for most busy people is that their work demands more than one-third of each day. Where do they find these extra hours? It seems logical that the extra work hours would come from those set aside for refreshment, but most successful individuals don't regularly reduce hours in this category. They are far too busy with other activities. Rather than giving up time from civic involvement, church participation, or club duties, extra time required from work is taken from the eight-hour period allotted for rest. These people conclude that somehow the time will come when they catch up on missed sleep, correcting the cumulative imbalance of weeks, months, and, for many, even years.

A major problem with such an approach is that it runs counter to that sage advice contending we should avoid "burning the candle at both ends." Not only are far too many of us guilty of taking on too much so that we overextend ourselves—but lacking the good sense to extinguish the flame at one end of the candle, we cry out for more wax! Yet, our energy levels are not infinite. There is only a certain amount of energy available, and any energy reserve can be exhausted, as far too many have sadly learned.

Often our judgments suffer when we've heaped too much abuse on our bodies. This was clearly depicted in the movie *High Noon,* where the law officer, as portrayed by Gary Cooper, was given an ultimatum to "leave town by noon." After several sleepless nights, Cooper was urged by his assistant to get on his mount and leave before the desperadoes returned. Almost persuaded, Cooper surprised his aid at the last moment by refusing to leave. His deputy questioned,

"But you said you were leaving?" to which Cooper replied, "Yes, I did, but I was tired then, and man will do a lot of foolish things when he's tired."

Sometimes it is necessary to shorten rest in order to accomplish more, but this should not go on indefinitely. In controlling our time, we need to make better use of our waking hours, for most of us waste far more time than we are willing to admit. Dr. Douglas Southall Freeman, the late editor of the *Richmond News Leader,* recognized this so well that he had a plaque placed on his desk which read: "Time alone is irreplaceable; waste it not."

Dr. Freeman wanted to do some permanent writing in addition to his work on the newspaper, but little time was available. Active in his community, he served as president of the board of the University of Richmond, in addition to holding positions on boards of other institutions, charities, and in civic enterprises. He was a gifted public speaker who made over a hundred speaking engagements annually.

One day a week he went to New York, where he lectured in Columbia University's School of Journalism. On another day he could be found in Washington, where he lectured. at the old Army War College. How did he ever find the necessary time to write seriously? On evenings when he had no speaking engagements he went to bed at eight o'clock. By 3:15 a.m. he was up, preparing his own breakfast. By 4 a.m. he was at his editor's desk, reading dispatches and writing editorials. While the rest of the city was just getting up, he was on the air delivering his daily radio news commentary. All morning he was at his editorial desk, breaking at noon for a second news commentary. It was after a fifteen-minute nap in the afternoon that he did his serious research and writing. In these hours which he carved from his heavy schedule, Dr. Freeman wrote his monumental volumes on George Washington and Robert E. Lee, ranked among the finest biographies ever written. Freeman always insisted that a person who would keep from wasting time could do just about anything he wished. Certainly Freeman was one of those rare individuals who met the opportunities of time and life by making time *serve* life.

Of course, few of us could get along with as little sleep as Dr. Freeman did. Most of us would require far more. Eight hours of daily rest and sleep is generally thought of as necessary to perform at peak efficiency, though individual biological clocks differ considerably in the amount of time regularly required for rest and sleep.

A definite link between longevity and moderation in living habits has been reported by Dr. Nedia B. Belloc of the California Health Department's Human Population Laboratory. Since 1965 a study has been run on 7,000 California residents concluding that men who follow the "seven golden rules of behavior" will live eleven years longer than those who do not. For women following these same seven rules, the increased life expectancy is seven years.

These proposed seven rules are straight forward and relatively simple. They include (1) eating regularly, but not between meals; (2) beginning each day with breakfast, a meal many forego; (3) getting eight hours of sleep on a regular rather than an occasional basis; (4) maintaining normal weight, being neither overweight nor underweight; (5) not smoking, or having stopped for a sufficient number of years so that the lung tissue has repaired itself; (6) drinking moderately, not more than one or two alcoholic beverages a day, if you drink at all, and (7) exercising regularly and sufficiently so that the body is kept in good shape. Dr. Lester Breslow, dean of the School of Public Health at the University of California at Los Angeles, claims, "The daily habits of people have a great deal more to do with what makes them sick, and when they will die, than all the influences of medicine."

Only after adequately meeting the more basic physiological needs can we proceed to a higher-order need such as social interaction, which is the subject of the next chapter.

·3·

No One Is an Island

Just as no one can totally live unto himself, hardly any of us would want to spend our entire lives with only one other person! At first such a notion might sound romantic, depending on the imagined partner, but soon such romanticism would give way to reality, as we recognize that no one individual can meet all our needs. Humans are complicated with needs which are too many and too diverse to be met by only one other person.

A distinction should be made at the outset between interacting superficially or in-depth with another. Superficial relationships, for example, are the kinds we have with our acquaintances as opposed to close friends. Surface relationships obviously require less than deeper interactions, but at the same time these superficial exchanges are also less fulfilling. Some people find less distress when they are away from home, where the relationships are less intense. This is really not surprising when you think about it.

A visitor in a small town was once asked by a leading citizen to join him for a game of golf. Later that evening the visitor was introduced to the wife of his host on the course that day. In elated tones the visitor exclaimed, "That husband of yours is one of the finest men I have ever met. Why today he took me to his club, insisted on paying all green fees, had me tee off first on each hole, regardless of who had won the preceding one, and even bought lunch and post-game drinks in the clubhouse after our round. I just want you to know how grateful I am to have met one so considerate as your husband. You must count yourself a most fortunate woman!" The wife looked wide-eyed at the visitor and replied, "Harry? You're talking about *my* Harry?" In those few words the visitor was told far more about Harry than would have been learned had he played golf with Harry every day for a year. Obviously Harry did not show the same regard for family members' feelings at home as he did for others when away. Charity may begin at home, as the Bible suggests, but it is far too easy for most of us to think of charity as starting in someone else's home. How we treat others in the most intimate relationships of life is far more important than the way we treat passing acquaintances.

The deeper psychological needs (addressed in the next chapter) can be met only when there is mutual respect present in the interpersonal interaction pattern. In a very real sense the individual who is more considerate, happier, and kinder outside the home is a fraud. Not only does the individual recognize this, but the most significant others in his or her life also know. Popeye's assertion, "I yam what I yam!" doesn't fit. Instead, such a person is keenly aware, "I yam what I yam *on occasion,*" and this makes it especially difficult for those with whom he or she is closest. Obviously the whole picture is needed to really understand an individual situation.

Such was the case involving the Pennsylvania Dutch farmer, who was suing a truck driver in court for having run him off the road when he was leading Bessie, his cow, to market. The attorney for the trucking firm had the farmer on the witness stand in court, attempting to destroy the farmer's credibility since the farmer claimed to have been hurt in the accident. The attorney inquired, "Didn't you tell my client immediately after the wreck that you *weren't* hurt?"

The farmer looked at the judge and began, "I was leading Bessie to market when this truck careened out of control and went crash..." The attorney broke in, saying, "All I want is a yes-or-no answer to my question. Isn't it true that you told my client immediately after the wreck that you weren't hurt?"

Again, the farmer began, "I was leading Bessie to market when this truck careened out of control and went crash..." The attorney glanced at the judge for support but the judge shrugged as if to imply, "We might as well hear out this old farmer."

The farmer continued, "...Knocking Bessie and me into a ditch. The truck driver got, came over, and peered down into the ditch where he could plainly see old Bessie was badly hurt. Returning to his truck, he removed his rifle from the gun rack, came back, and with a single shot put Bessie out of her misery. Then with the gun still smoking, he turned to me lying there in the ditch where I had been thrown and asked, 'Are you hurt?' Now how would you have responded?" inquired the farmer of the twelve jurors. This story simply illustrates that in our dealings with other people, we need to have in-depth relationships before we really understand their behavior and their feelings.

For example, one of the greatest problems faced by many is loneliness. However, not only the widowed, divorced, or single are lonely—some of the loneliest people are married! In writing the syndicated column, "Families Under Stress," one of the subjects readers frequently address is loneliness. It never ceases to amaze me that so many married people are so lonely. Once they marry, they believe their lonely years are behind them, little realizing that in too many instances, a different kind of loneliness lies ahead.

Often it seems that both males and females are guilty of assuming that once the chase (courtship stage) is completed, the race (interpersonal relationship) has been won. Yet, everyone is constantly changing, and these changes must be accommodated if two individuals are to grow together. Loneliness occurs when one or both mates are unwilling to invest themselves further in pursuing the other. Withdrawal takes over, each assuming that it is up to the other to make the relationship successful.

Further, this belief becomes cemented as one (or both) partner faults the other for the qualities which he most dislikes in himself. This defense mechanism is known as *projection,* where we attempt to rid ourselves of undesirable traits by attributing them to another, thus freeing us from any real responsibility for failure in the interpersonal relationship.

This defense mechanism needs to be guarded against, because it is natural to use when relationships become strained. Not wanting to assume responsibility for difficulties encountered in the relationship, we make our partners the scapegoats. As is usually the case, there is always just enough logic present to support our irrational belief that the other is totally, or nearly totally, to blame. If we will look honestly within ourselves we will be aware that each person plays a vital role if the relationship is to succeed, for though one individual can break a relationship, one person can *never* make it succeed. This is the most important truth necessary to establish a firm base within marriage, which, in turn, equips us to welcome stress.

Sociologically, we tend to marry people like ourselves, as first pointed out by Hollingshead in his article, "Cultural Factors in the Selection of Marriage Mates," in the *American Sociological Review*. Most of us select mates of our own racial composition, from similar educational and socioeconomic backgrounds, and in the same age category (plus or minus five years). This is known as the sociological theory of homogamy, i.e., "like attracts like." Paradoxically, the psychological theory of heterogamy, i.e., "opposites attract opposites" also applies when we choose our mates. When we think of the personality types we find most attractive, it becomes readily apparent that we are not attracted to those personalities similar to our own but rather to those who are different, who complement us. The submissive person is thus (for example) attracted to the more dominant individual, otherwise conflict would loom large in a relationship where each person has similar needs. Neither would be free to fulfill the needs of the other.

Cardiologists Drs. Meyer Friedman and Ray H. Rosenman first became aware of similar personality patterns in patients they were treating when an upholstery repairman remarked how strange it was that only the front edge of the chairs in their waiting room were worn out. They began to formalize a personality theory designating two primary personality patterns, Type A and Type B. An awareness of characteristics of these two types is most important to understanding and interacting with others.

How can you tell if you are a Type A personality? Take a moment to assess yourself using the checklist in the following Stress Inventory IV.

Stress Inventory IV
Type A Profile*

Check all following self-descriptive statements:

_____ Speak the last few words of your sentence rapidly.

_____ Always move, walk, and eat rapidly.

_____ Feel impatient with rate at which most events take place.

_____ Usually attempt to finish others' sentences.

_____ Become unduly irritated when traffic is slow.

_____ Find it intolerable to watch others do tasks you could do faster.

_____ Usually look for summaries of interesting literature.

_____ Indulge in polyphasic thought, trying to think of or do two or more things simultaneously.

_____ Ponder business problems while away from the office.

_____ Pretend to listen to others but remain preoccupied with your own thoughts.

_____ Almost always feel vaguely guilty when you relax.

_____ Don't take time to appreciate surroundings, i.e., sunsets, scenic beauty, etc.

_____ Attempt to schedule more and more in less and less time.

_____ Possess a chronic sense of time urgency.

_____ Feel compelled to challenge another like yourself.

_____ Recognize aggressive behavior in yourself which may not be noticed by others.

_____ Frequently clench fist in conversation.

_____ Bang your hand upon a table or pound one fist into palm of other in order to emphasize a point.

_____ Habitually clench your jaw or grind your teeth.

_____ Believe your success has been due to your ability to get things done faster than others.

_____ Evaluate your own and others' activities in terms of numbers.

_____ Total

Key: Total the number of checks made above. If there are seven or fewer, there is little likelihood you are a Type A personality; seven to twelve checks indicate a tendency toward a Type A personality structure, while more than twelve suggest you are a Type A personality.

*Adapted from Friedman, Meyer and Rosenman, Ray H., *Type A Behavior and Your Heart.* New York: Fawcett Crest, 1974.

Type A personalities are life's drivers, the hard-ball players, intense, aggressive, and ambitious. They love competition and constantly operate under tremendous pressure to get things done. Impatient, they usually balk at standing in line for anything, steaming when caught in traffic jams or while waiting for slow-moving clerks. Time is their constant enemy, something to be fought and raced against. These people speak with machine-gun rapidity, tend to live highly disciplined lives, end sentences in a rush, interrupt others in mid-sentence, and often sigh faintly between words due to exhaustion from stress.

There is no time to get sick nor to relax even when on a vacation. Vacations are always crammed with activities, never planned as restful interludes from usual hectic schedules. Even games are played with a constant determination to win rather than participated in as a source of enjoyment. Preoccupation with work dominates their lives, as they rush through the present with a constant eye on the future. Never is the present enjoyed for itself, because attention is riveted on what is to come. The Type A person hurries through the evening meal, thinking about the meeting scheduled later that night, only to sit through the meeting with the mind focusing on what's to be done at work tomorrow.

Most people polled would probably agree that Type A personalities are the ones who succeed in life—these are the corporation presidents, the high-level executives who become "kings of the hill" in their respective fields. However, research suggests that Type A's often lose out to Type B's for promotion, as the former are *too* competitive, compulsive, and make decisions too rapidly without considering all the facts. Studies show that the more successful executives are those who are more deliberate and creative. Greatest emphasis is placed not on the number of calls, or contracts, but rather on the more substantive issues confronting the firm's future. Obviously these individuals are more valuable as chief executive officers than are the uptight, hurried, and often harried Type A's.

Can Type A behavior be learned? In the home or on the job, most of us are susceptible to mimicking others' behavior. At home this may occur as a result of our desire to please, yet on-the-job workers may assume this is the only behavior that will lead to success. Of course Type A behavior can be both productive and desirable under the proper conditions. However, if we are not already Type A personalities, we need to avoid absorbing some of the worst features of that personality from those close to us.

How many of the following personality traits common to Type A's do you recognize in the most significant others in your life, or indeed, in yourself?

1. *Intense sense of time urgency.* This is the trait which drives the individual to race against the clock, even when there is little reason to do so, as if the goal is to hurry for the sake of hurrying. Setting goals to complete tasks in less and less time is a hallmark of Type A behavior.

2. *Inappropriate aggression and hostility.* The Type A personality is excessively competitive. Few activities are done for the fun of it. Because aggressive behavior is required to remain constantly competitive, the line is easily crossed from aggressiveness to hostility. Often hostility will be displayed at the slightest provocation or frustration.

3. *Polyphasic behavior.* This is an educated phrase for doing two or more things at the same time. Sometimes this is necessary, but when the individual is *constantly* attempting to accomplish more than one task at a time, the behavior is inappropriate. Frequently the result is wasted time. The old adage "Haste makes waste" is appropriate here. So is the newer slogan: "If I don't take time to do it right right now, when will I find time to do it over?"

4. *Goal direction without proper planning.* This happens when one rushes to start the job without first determining the best procedures. Soon changes in the approach become necessary as the worker learns the best method through trial and error rather than as a result of proper planning. Not only is time wasted, but the outcome is costly, as well.

The Type B personality finds it easier to "hang loose" emotionally, is capable of hard work but shifts gears successfully, leaving work to enjoy diverse activities. This worker is not a clock-watcher, attempting to perform all tasks in less and less time, but places emphasis on *quality* in daily living. Being first in everything is not nearly so important as for the Type A personality. This personality finds it far easier to delegate responsibility and does not feel that time taken out to think and become more creative is wasted. These people can relax and not feel guilty, frequently enjoying aspects of life that are *not* work-oriented.

Invariably the question is asked, "Can Type A personalities be changed?" The answer is, "Yes, but they must *want* to change." A reader of my syndicated column wrote asking how she could get her husband to drop some of his bothersome Type A behaviors in favor of healthier Type B traits. She ended with the plaintive plea, "How can I get him to change if he doesn't want to?"

First, assuming her husband is strong-willed, it will be impossible to force him to change. Until he feels a need to change, all her efforts will not alter his behavior. Therefore, his reasons for resisting any change in unhealthy habits must be examined at the outset.

Of course a Type A personality can become a Type B if he or she can let go of the need to be compulsive. The danger is that if people are unwillingly reformed to Type B, they may substitute activities which seem characteristic of Type B, but not really change their personalities at all.

Consider the example of a reformed Type A who decides to relax and enjoy nature. Suppose he decides to take a refreshing walk in the woods, soaking up the beauty and splendor about him. In actuality he becomes engrossed in making lists of all the different birds he can identify! Next he sets up an exacting schedule, determined to identify more birds each day, more today than yesterday, more tomorrow than today, eventually identifying more birds per day than anyone ever thought possible. His goal will be to become not only a champion bird watcher, but the most disciplined practitioner of such Type B activities in existence! As you can see, he really hasn't changed his personality at all.

So much for Type A personalities becoming Type B's unless they are motivated to change. Still, we must never lose sight of the possibility of laying groundwork causing the individual to *want* to change. Igniting a spark from within will be far more effective in bringing about change than any external condition imposed.

Why is change so difficult for most of us? Leaving the familiar poses problems for many people, because they are far more comfortable with the known past than the unknown future. Drs. Holmes and Rahe devised a Life Change Unit Rating which helps us note the differences in various changes as they affect our lives. Their scale is presented here as Stress Inventory V.

Stress Inventory V
Life Change Unit Rating*

Enter the total points beside each change in the column category "Yours" for any of these changes that have occurred in your life in the past year. Total the "Yours" column for a grand total of your own Life Change Unit Rating.

Work Events	Life Change Units	Yours
Fired from work	47	_____
Retired	45	_____
Major business adjustment	39	_____
Change to different line of work	36	_____
Change in responsibilities at work	29	_____
Trouble with boss	23	_____
Change in work hours or conditions	20	_____

Personal

Major personal injury or illness	53	_____
Outstanding personal achievement	28	_____
Change in recreation	19	_____
Revision of personal habits	24	_____
Change in church activities	19	_____
Change in sleeping habits	16	_____
Change in eating habits	15	_____
Vacation	13	_____
Christmas	12	_____

Financial

Change in financial state	38	_____
Mortgage or loan for major purchase (home, etc.)	31	_____

Foreclosure of mortgage or loan	30	_____
Mortgage or loan for lesser purchase (car, TV, etc.)	17	_____

Family

Death of a spouse	100	_____
Divorce	73	_____
Marital separation	65	_____
Death of a close family member	63	_____
Marriage	50	_____
Marital reconciliation	45	_____
Change in health of family member	44	_____
Pregnancy	40	_____
Gain of a new family member	39	_____
Change in number of arguments with spouse	35	_____
Son or daughter leaving home	29	_____
Troubles with in-laws	29	_____
Spouse starting or ending work	26	_____
Change in number of family get-togethers	15	_____

Social

Jail term	63	_____
Sex difficulties	39	_____
Death of a close friend	37	_____
Start or end of formal schooling	26	_____
Major change in living conditions	25	_____
Changing to a new school	20	_____
Change in residence	20	_____
Change in social activities	18	_____
Minor violations of the law	11	_____
	Total:	_____

*Holmes, T. H. and Rahe, R. H. "The Social Readjustment Rating Scale," *Journal of Psychosomatic Research.* (1967) 11:213-218.

As a guide to what your score means, compare your results with the following study. Using the Holmes and Rahe scale, researchers Culligan and Sedlack measured Seattle residents over a two-year period.[1] After two years, 86 percent of the subjects scoring over 300 points (in a one-year period) on the Life Change Scale experienced major illnesses. Of those scoring between 150 and 300 points, 48 percent became ill, while only 33 percent of those scoring less than 150 points experienced a health change.

This suggests the following scale indicating the potential for good health based on the number of significant changes in your life within one year:

Less than 150 points	Good
151 to 300 points	Fair
More than 300 points	Poor

Of course, change cannot be avoided — life is a series of constant changes. The issue then is not, "How can I *avoid* change?" — but rather "How can I *cope* with change?"

To begin with, some change can be eliminated in any life. In addition, there is good reason not to compound change. The widow or widower is best advised not to compound change by undertaking a major move (20 points) within the year following the death of a spouse (100 points). Likewise, the newly married (50 points) would be wise to avoid pregnancy (40 points) in the first year of marriage. Though we cannot eliminate change, we can lessen its impact so that its effects are not so stressful.

Stress has many other sociological sources. Inflation, recession, and unemployment — all cause mental strain. Unemployment is a killer disease, so significant is society's expectation that each individual should be gainfully employed. Work is at the center of life for many; the longer the period of unemployment, the larger the number of expected antisocial symptoms occur, such as child abuse, alcoholism, sexual infertility, and even physical ailments.

Another battering force coming down more heavily on us now is the successive years of double-digit inflation. Older persons can relate to the Depression as a frame of reference. Recalling this era is so painful for most that these memories create a great deal of anxiety and mental depression. Also, younger people are fearful that they cannot continue to afford their accustomed standard of living. Many are extremely anxious, seeing little hope of keeping abreast of inflation.

Inflation, when combined with other life stresses, can completely overwhelm those who are prone to anxiety. Dr. M. Harvey Brenner, a John Hopkins University sociologist and an expert in the field of money problems and mental illness, asks and then answers, "Can inflation drive you crazy? When you add it to existing pressures, yes."

Does this mean that all change is socially undesirable? Of course not! A reduction in the number of teenage pregnancies, fewer alcoholics, controlling or preventing the antisocial behavior of street-wise adolescents who prey on the elderly and poor—these are but a few changes that would be beneficial.

Dr. Miller Upton, president of Beloit College in Beloit, Wisconsin, made a strong case for encouraging beneficial change when he addressed students at an honors convocation, stating:

> I have just about reached the end of my tolerance for
> the way our society now seems to have sympathetic
> concern only for the misfit, the pervert, the drug
> addict, the drifter, the chronic criminal, and the
> underachiever. It seems to me that we have lost touch

with reality and become warped in our attachments. I feel it is time for someone like me to stand up and say, in short, "I'm for the upperdog!" I am for the achiever—the one who sets out to do something and does it; the one who recognizes the problems and opportunities at hand, and endeavors to deal with them; the one who is successful at his immediate task because he is not worrying about someone else's failings; the one who doesn't consider it "square" to be constantly looking for more to do, who isn't always rationalizing why he shouldn't be doing what he is doing; the one, in short, who carries the work of his part of the world squarely on his shoulders. It is important to recognize that the quality of any society is directly related to the quality of the individuals who make it up. Therefore, let us stop referring naively to creating a "great society." It is enough, at this stage of our development, to aspire to create a decent society. To do so, our first task is to help each individual be decent unto himself and in his relationship with other individuals. We will never create a good society, much less a great one, until individual excellence and achievement are not only respected but encouraged. That is why I am for the upperdog—the achiever—the succeeder.

If society is to encourage its "upperdogs," there must be a return to valuing discipline as one of life's most prized components.

Socrates observed that the unexamined life is not worth living. If we were to substitute the term "undisciplined" for "unexamined," the statement would be just as true, for the undisciplined life brings joy neither to the individual nor to those who must tolerate his assumed license to respect no living creature, not even himself.

Human behavior is a complex subject. No behavior just happens; *all behavior has a cause.* Take the case of the

46

teenager who refuses to do his school work, choosing instead to annoy others. What causes such behavior and what can be done about it?

Psychological possibilities for his acting in this manner may consist of insecurity plus a need to seek attention, even when the attention is negative; a low self-concept which continually needs raising at almost any cost, hence his lack of concern if his teachers are upset; hostility towards those in authority; lack of parental support for education; or a host of other reasons.

More importantly, what can we do as parents to encourage self-discipline on the part of our children? Usually this is a process which begins in early childhood.

Have you ever said, "I want my child to have it easier," or "I hope my child will never have to work as hard as I did"? These are common statements from parents who think they are acting in their children's best interests. But are they *really?* Children suffer when parents do things for them they should be doing for themselves. In the name of love, parents are actually crippling their children by taking over and doing those tasks a child could do. The children must learn to help themselves. Childhood is a time for learning. If children are not permitted to make many attempts—some of which will result in failure—then they are deprived of valuable learning experiences. The danger is that they will grow up poorly equipped to survive, simply because they were never taught the art of survival, like the pelicans in the following story.

For years, at a seaside commercial fishery, after cleaning the day's catch, the men threw the fish refuse back into the water. Pelicans swarmed over the water, enjoying this effortless food bonanza. When the fishery closed, the pelicans began to die from starvation. They had never learned to use their beaks to catch their daily food supply. Seeking a solution, biologists trapped pelicans from other locations, releasing them to join the local pelicans dying of starvation. Then an amazing thing happened: a large portion of the native pelicans survived. Why? Because they learned to fish by imitating the imported pelicans who had never been deprived of finding and catching their own food.

The lesson is obvious. If our children are to compete effectively in a world which is expected to be even more complex than the one we have known, they will need all the help they can get. Children will encounter stress, but all stress need not lead to distress for children who have successfully been prepared during their childhood years to face life's demands.

Many doom criers would have us believe that the American family, the cornerstone of our society, is falling apart. Far from it! Recognizing and grappling with weaknesses in the family systems are precisely what will make them strong enough to survive, perhaps becoming even stronger than before.

Shrill voices have excitedly proclaimed, "The American family is on its deathbed and the patient has lost its will to survive!" However, this simply isn't true, as the following study attests. Sociologist Theodore Caplow, director of an extension of the 1924 study "Middletown, U.S.A.," concluded that while there are symptoms of torn fabric of family life, i.e., the isolation of the nuclear family, high divorce rate, the widening generation gap, the loss of parental authority, the general dissatisfaction with marriage, and the weakening influence of religion, there is also evidence of increased family solidarity, a smaller generation gap, closer marital communication, more religion, and less mobility. He concluded that these changes reflect a strengthening of the family as an institution, with corresponding increased satisfaction with the family.

Sociologically, the family is strong, and predictions of its demise—which abounded only a decade ago—seem as foolish today as the "God Is Dead" movement of more than twenty years ago. Of course, the family will continue to experience stress, but these stresses when confronted rather than avoided will strengthen the family as a unit. Consequently, families, as well as individuals, can learn to welcome stress!

·4·

Mind Over Stressful Matter

There is no question that human stress must be studied as an integrated whole, i.e., the holistic approach. The emotions are affected and in turn affect physiological responses in the body, as becomes apparent when man is viewed from a psychological perspective. Only in recent years has emotional stress been understood as a primary cause of physical illnesses. As stated previously, the Dutch physician, the late Dr. Hans Selye, pioneered in recognizing the causal relationship between stress and illness. In responding to stress of any type, the whole body reacts with what he terms a "General Adaptation Syndrome."

Indeed research has emphasized anew the need to integrate the parts into a whole, with each major area interdependent on the others. This was reported most recently by Harvard researchers who discovered the tiny double knot of cells in the brain which control the body's pace.

In their experiments with monkeys, Drs. Lydic, Schoone, Czeisler, and Moore discovered a tiny knot of brain cells which monitors the resting, drinking, eating, and other activities, permitting these primates to follow a predictable daily schedule. Using microsurgical techniques, they destroyed this tiny pacemaker spot in the monkey's brain with an electrode needle. The pattern of rest and activity quickly disintegrated, and although the same amount of waking, sleeping, eating, and drinking took place, all regularity was lost.

These scientists have located a comparable bundle of nerves in the human brain controlling the sleep-wake cycle. This is one of the two major pacemakers in humans, the other governing the body's temperature rhythm. The two interact, affecting blood pressure which varies by as much as twenty-five points over a day, limiting daily cell-division rate changes by 1,200 percent, permitting the observation that a person is both biologically and psychologically a different creature at different times of the day. Abilities of all types, most notably performance on intelligence tests, were observed to vary greatly with the body's daily cycles.

Recognition of the interdependence of the mind and body is not new. Many ancient writers made reference to ways the mind affects the body. What remains a great mystery is how emotional concern *causes* physical illnesses. The central nervous system within the body is influenced by *all* experiences. Following family arguments, most of us become emotionally upset. We may act and react with anger, resentment, hostility, and guilt, which can continue even after the matter has been consciously forgotten. Subconsciously the mind continues working, slow to free us from repercussions following these confrontations.

Often we experience negative side effects long after a difficult encounter. "Out of sight—out of mind" doesn't apply to stress resulting from arguments, because whatever caused stress in the first place may remain in our thoughts long after the incident. When experiencing any emotional upheaval, the entire body responds with physical effects. This is most readily recognized when we are in love.

Love is probably the most widely misused word in our language. We use it to describe man's feelings toward his Creator, sweetheart, all family members, friends (to say nothing of acquaintances), and many material items. A man will say, "I love my car," while a woman exclaims, "I just love your dress, dear," whether sincere or not.

The best and most plausible definition of love was stated by Dr. Harry Sullivan, founder of the Washington School of Psychiatry: *love is that condition which exists when you are as interested in fulfilling the needs of another as you are in having your own fulfilled.*

Most of us feel and express love for our mates, children, parents, close friends, and even our pets. There are different levels or kinds of love felt for our parents as opposed to our children. Of course in the best family relationships, the strongest bond of love will exist between husband and wife.

However, even the best marriages require constant re-inforcement. This is not to suggest that such love is inherently weak, but rather that a deeply felt love will constantly seek ways to express itself, demanding much from both parties. Mates must work continually at building and renewing their relationships or their ability to meet each other's needs is questionable, for marriage is comparable to a bicycle: when left to coast, it will do so for a short while, but then only if it's downhill!

Ending a love relationship is always stressful. Making the transition from "in love" to "out of love" isn't easy, but it needn't be as traumatic as it sometimes becomes. Drs. Debora Phillips and Robert Judd in *How to Fall Out of Love* contend that there are systematic steps which can be followed enabling one to stop thinking of a particular person by crumbling the romantic image of the other person. For instance, silent ridicule is a method of learning to laugh at someone instead of worshiping him or her. This requires a psychological shift from hostility to indifference, and though difficult, it is possible to achieve. This underscores Dr. Rollo May's assertion, "The opposite of love isn't hate, but indifference." Negative thoughts will be replaced by neutral or even positive ones as this is accomplished.

Like love, worry also generates stress. "Nothing in the affairs of men is worth worrying about," wrote Plato, but his advice is ignored by many. We worry about a variety of things, though common to most of our worries is the fear that others will see them as unfounded. It is important to control worry, for it is damaging to one's health. Not only does it affect circulation, the heart, and the glands, but the whole nervous system. Dr. Charles Mayo once said, "I have never known a man who died from overwork, but many who died from overworry."

Worry takes over when reason is sidetracked. If you examine your situation, you will probably discover that worry occurs when you cease thinking about the facts and focus on the way you *feel* about what happened. Feelings are subjective, leaving you free to imagine all kinds of things. For example, separated spouses conjure up many conceivable notions as to why their children rejected them for the other parent.

There is little difference between past worry and present concern over future possibilities. If every imagined possibility were to come true, our worrying would be legitimate. Or if worrying itself could prevent the worst from happening, it could be justified. However, seldom does the worst occur, and furthermore worry is habit-forming. When one is worried, the temptation is to mull over negative possibilities of pending situations. To put emphasis on possible positive outcomes requires work, for we must give ourselves good reasons for thinking positively. Negative thinking requires no substantiation.

One of our worst mistakes is to examine problems either when we are tired or awake in the middle of the night. When tired, our defenses are down; we do not possess sufficient resources to view problems realistically. If not careful, we are lured into practicing emotional brinkmanship, where we race to the edge of the emotional precipice, entertaining the loss of our most prized possession, only then pulling back to a safer emotional comfort zone.

This kind of thinking is reminiscent of the ancient tale, where shortly after the engaged couple was seated with her family for dinner, she rose from the table to go down to the cellar and fetch preserves to accompany the meal. Because she was gone so long, her fiance excused himself, going off to search for her. He found her sitting on the cellar steps, dissolved in tears. Asking her, "What's the matter?" she pointed to a hatchet carelessly hung from an overhead beam, explaining, "Suppose after we marry and have a child, our child comes running down here on an errand some day and the hatchet slips from its hook, killing her instantly!" The tale concluded with the man sitting down beside his intended, whereupon both of them become overwrought reflecting on this future possibility.

Although there is an obvious absence of logic in this story, most of our concerns over future possibilities are no more rational. We are able to see the folly in another's anxiety when we are not emotionally entangled, yet when we are emotionally involved, our vision is not as clear.

A combination of exhaustion and darkness may cause worry to shift from anxiety to panic. Darkness always magnifies our alarm. Noises heard in a house go unnoticed during the day, but these same rumblings at night cause fear in the hearts of even the brave. We need to refuse to dwell on worries either late at night or when exhausted. As worries approach the threshold of the mind, we can be effective traffic cops, turning them away and resolving that we will confront them first thing in the morning.

Of course everyone experiences feelings of anxiety, uncertainty, and apprehension—these are normal. However, when one reacts disproportionately to the stresses being experienced, real anxiety disorders result.

Psychologically there are two distinct types of anxiety disorders: (1) generalized anxiety, a state of chronic apprehension and tension, and (2) anxiety distinguished by panic attacks. The latter occurs when people suddenly become overwhelmed, fearing some kind of loss of control.

Although therapy can be very helpful in dealing with anxiety, there are additional ways to cope more effectively, beginning with the recognition that *everyone has problems.* Though this won't lessen the importance of personal problems, it does help to put the ordeal in perspective. Never forget that your body gears up in response to difficulties with an extra spurt of energizing power, enabling you to cope adequately during troubled times.

Next, remember that only *rarely will events turn out as badly as you fear.* Reflecting on your worst fears of the past, which of them have come true? Probably very few, so don't waste time conjuring up the worst scenario. Seldom is life quite as bad as we imagine!

Above all, *don't spend time feeling sorry for yourself!* This is a luxury we cannot afford. Most of us ultimately receive from others in life pretty much what we deserve. This doesn't mean that by living a good life we will avoid all heartache, but regardless of our burdens, the really important things in life are usually there when needed. These include love, respect, friendship, and even peace—so work at deserving these important things in life.

When you feel panic coming on, don't become inactive or go off by yourself. You need to keep active, changing your environment if possible. A different location, even briefly, can be therapeutic. See as many of your friends as possible. Talk over any real concern with those you trust or with others important in your life such as your clergyman, doctor, or lawyer.

If sleep is elusive, *don't waste time lying in bed worrying about not being able to sleep.* Get up and read, play music, or write that letter you have been meaning to send. Some patients of mine have found momentary relief in reading fiction as a form of escape from the immediate press of panic.

Finally, and perhaps most important, *refuse to become the center of your universe.* Reach out and help others! There is a cleansing, uplifting quality found in helping others, enabling us to put life in its proper perspective.

Coping successfully with the stress from anxiety helps free one to live life at its best. Similarly, dealing with unresolved anger helps avoid rage. Rage, generally caused by anxiety from intense, pent-up, hostile feelings, builds up over a long period of time. Finally, some incident — perhaps an insignificant one — triggers an explosive release of the suppressed anger, often culminating in hostile acts.

Seldom is the reaction in proportion to the incident triggering the episode. This is where someone usually refers to "the straw that broke the camel's back," but what we need to remember is that it is never just a single straw, but the weight of all the other straws that causes the proverbial broken back of the camel.

Police officers often encounter rage when called in on domestic disorders. This is why most officers fear domestic fights more than any other disturbance. Emotions involved in pent-up anger with one's mate may break forth in what is not inappropriately described as a "fit of rage," with the enraged partner responding violently and unpredictably.

Though rage may be triggered by either alcohol or other drugs, it also arises simply because the individual has reached a point where he or she cannot deal with further frustration. Rage can be short-circuited, subsiding long before the enraged person inflicts harm on either himself or others. To do this we must deal openly with anger rather than permit it to fester within us. Communication skills are crucial in dealing with defusing the cause of rage, for if a person is able to express anger verbally as it arises, there will be less likelihood of a base of rage from which mayhem or murder can occur.

Another manifestation of distress is depression. Anxiety and depression are frequently seen in the same patients. As with any disorder, early recognition and treatment afford the best prognosis.

Depression can be categorized three ways: (1) mild, (2) moderate, or (3) severe. Many people falsely believe that depression is not real unless it is severe. Often depression is not recognized by the one depressed because there is seemingly no valid reason to feel that way.

Stress Inventory VI
Symptoms of Stress

Check each of the following which you experience with some degree of frequency.

_____ Fatigue

A depressed person tires easily. Previous levels of energy may have diminished appreciably.

_____ Insomnia

While sleep may be intensely desired, it is elusive once the individual has retired for the evening. A similar condition is noted when one regularly awakens early with feelings of exhaustion or fright.

_____ Inability to concentrate

After watching a television program, listening to a lecture or even participating in a conversation, little content can be recalled.

_____ Remorse

Guilt is frequently noted in the depressed person, arising over either acts of commission or omission.

_____ Indecision

Many depressed people cannot make up their minds about anything. Even the simplest decisions seem too difficult for them.

_____ Decreased affection

It may come as a surprise, but the depressed person may feel little affection towards those much loved in the past.

_____	Reduced sexual interest	The depressed individual may have little interest in participating in sexual relations.
_____	Anxiety	Depression may be accompanied by feelings of tension, anxiety, or fright. Sometimes these feelings are so strong that they mask their underlying cause—depression.
_____	Irritability	The depressed person is easily annoyed and impatient, particularly over trivial things.
_____	Thoughts of suicide	Occasional thoughts of suicide are not uncommon in the depressed person. Fortunately, these ideas disappear when the individual starts to feel better but if they persist, indicate a need for immediate professional help.
_____	Concern about dying	Hardly a paradox following the mention of suicide, fearfulness of imminent death may be another symptom of depression. In actuality, both a concern with dying and suicide are frequently noted in the same depressed individual.

Note: Rating depression with a numerical scale only suggests but does not diagnose the seriousness of the problem. In general, five or fewer checks indicate mild depression; six or seven moderate, and eight or more serious depression. Of course a seriously depressed person needs professional help. However, any person who feels that his or her depression is not manageable or is out of control should consult a therapist for treatment and/or referral.

What causes depression? Basically it results from a combination of an individual's susceptibility and the stress he or she encounters. Especially where loss occurs, whether it is of business, money, spouse through divorce, or family member via death, depression is common.

Depression may be "normal" or "abnormal," grief being an example of normal depression. When death strikes close to home, it is normal to have depressing thoughts. There may even be a temporary loss of interest in life, further distorted by a pessimistic view of the future. In most cases involving loss, depression is temporary, but should it become severe, an immediate need for treatment is indicated.

When depression is primarily "abnormal," psychotherapy is indicated. This kind of depression has no apparent, real, negative event causing it and is characterized by intense sadness, an inability to find joy in life, feelings of hopelessness, or a loss of interest in one's surroundings.

Everyone is prone to occasional depression, which is normal and should not cause alarm. When becoming anxious over personal depression, determine how long the depressed mood has been present. If the answer is more than a month, professional help, which is available in virtually all communities, should be sought. Meanwhile, alcohol and drugs, so-called "antidepressants," should definitely be avoided. The "cure," if any, will only result in a more serious relapse later.

Ferreting out factors contributing to "blue" or "down" feelings can help us control our stress levels, even making this stress work for us. How do you cope with frustration? When your path to a desired goal is blocked, how do you respond? Do you usually find solutions to your problems? Sometimes solutions are not so obvious, but every problem contains at least a portion of its own solution if we will only examine it closely.

Are you persistent in moving ahead in spite of a disappointing experience? This requires developing an outlook wherein you never accept defeat, especially concerning ultimate goals. A word of caution: rather than remaining rigid, attempting to force a particular method to work, we will do better to be flexible enough to maneuver around temporary obstacles in our paths, using different means to accomplish the original goal.

Withdrawal is an overworked defense mechanism luring each of us on occasion. When we get down or feel mildly depressed, it is tempting to go to bed in the middle of the day, relying on sleep to alleviate the present problem. However, even if sleep comes, it may not be merciful, because such sleep is too often only a fitful blanket of peace temporarily shielding the immediate problem from conscious thoughts. An active approach is better, focusing attention either on the problem at hand or on some other diversion for the moment. Activity usually permits us to work through anxiety symptoms and lessens tension accompanying a down mood.

The quickest way to forget your own problems is to become involved in doing something for another, but many of us lack the self-discipline necessary to do so, even if we expect it will be successful. The next time you feel a down or "blue" mood approaching, switch your thoughts to another by actively doing something for someone else. There is no better way of avoiding periods of mild depression, and it will most likely work — *provided* you make the effort.

How much control can individuals assert over their own lives? As much as they want! This is not to suggest man is in ultimate control, but rather that our ability to control or influence events in our lives undoubtedly has fewer limits than we imagine. One word seemingly makes all the difference:

A-T-T-I-T-U-D-E

If we constantly think negatively or anticipate dire consequences, we are tempted to give up, thereby contributing to the very outcome we feared most. Also, we tend to create the conditions we most wanted to avoid. One who fears failure will find that dwelling on its prospects will increase the chances of failure. For example, drivers who become overly concerned with the likelihood of having an accident actually increase their chances of having a wreck!

To succeed, we must have positive attitudes, refusing to give up, regardless of the temptation. People who keep going in spite of obstacles are exercising an inner strength which most possess, but few recognize. This resource provides us with the drive necessary to persist in spite of boredom or temporary setbacks.

If we permit pessimism to overcome us, we stifle creative attitudes. Of course there is no guarantee that optimistic persistence will lead to victory, but defeat *is* guaranteed if we permit pessimism to dominate our lives. A person's attitude has even been known to make the difference between life and death!

Several years ago Captain Eddie Rickenbacker was in a serious airplane crash near Atlanta. He was rushed to the hospital where he was expected to die. Lying there drifting in and out of consciousness, he heard the voice of Walter Winchell, announcing to his radio listeners, "Friends, pray for Eddie Richenbacker. He is dying in an Atlanta hospital. He is not expected to live through the night."

Upon hearing this, Rickenbacker heaved a pitcher of water from his bedside at the radio, stilling the announcement that he was dying. He thought, "I'm not going to die! I'm not going to give up!" This indomitable attitude helped Rickenbacker recover and return to a productive life. Had he been inclined to give up, he probably would have died, so severe were his injuries. Obviously one's attitude is not the only element involved in recovering from accident or illness, but attitude *is* important to any patient's recovery.

Just how important is attitude in terms of success? The late H. L. Hunt, one of the world's wealthiest men, was asked if there were any secrets to success. Mr. Hunt replied, "First, decide what you want; second, decide what you are willing to give up to get it; third, establish your priorities; and fourth, get on with your work." If you want to succeed, you must desire success so much that you are willing to make whatever sacrifices are necessary to achieve it. With such a commitment, there is no question but that you will succeed!

When preparing for success psychologically, several steps must be considered. These are noted in five key words:

Vividly
Ardently
Sincerely
Enthusiastically
Must

To formulate a goal you must VIVIDLY imagine it. Mentally picture the goal. Image it. Envision it until you see yourself having achieved it. For this process to work, you will have to ARDENTLY desire success. This requires that you persistently pursue the goal, letting nothing deter you from reaching it. Commitment is necessary if you are going to succeed. The next step requires that you SINCERELY believe in yourself and in your ability to achieve your goal.

Once you begin seeing yourself as having succeeded, others will view you similarly.

However, the first three steps would be in vain if no extraordinary action were taken. Therefore it is imperative that you ENTHUSIASTICALLY act upon making your goal become a reality. Enthusiasm is contagious! Too often we drag along, showing nothing that attracts or inspires others. If others are to help you achieve your goal—and the cooperation of others is usually vital to any program of success—it is necessary that they give you positive reinforcement as you strive toward achieving your goal.

Any goal toward which you apply all four of these principles MUST inevitably come to pass. This is not to suggest any magic, but rather to emphasize the importance your own attitude plays in reaching your goals. Dr. Karl Menninger said it best when he noted, "Attitude is always more important than fact!" So it is, especially in achieving success!

It is a risky business ever to underestimate the human mind. Admiral James Stockdale, one of our military men who was imprisoned longest as a POW in Vietnam, addressed a scientific group demonstrating the capability of the mind. He described how the mind can be expanded and trained by recalling codes used to communicate among POWs while in prison.

One of anything—a tap, bang on the wall, cough, or dropped cup—meant danger. The admiral recalled that the POWs couldn't be accused of anything by doing something only once. Two of anything meant yes, three repeat, and four wait. All of this was devised without the prisoners ever talking among themselves. They relied solely on mental imagery to control their attitudes and emotions.

Even more impressive was their five-by-five grid, containing all the letters of the alphabet with the exception of "k." Each letter could be identified by two sets of taps—one for its line and the other for its place in the line. Adding some one-, two-, or three-letter abbreviations, they had a method of communicating which defied the isolation of their confinement. "To be asked to sweep the courtyard was to be invited to give a public speech," said Admiral Stockdale, for with each swish of the broom the captive was able to "talk" to his fellow prisoners.

Another POW returning home after many years in prison scored lowest of his old golf foursome the first time back on the course. His friends were simply amazed, inquiring how he accounted for this feat when he had been imprisoned in a foreign country for many years while they had played golf twice a week on that same course.

He replied, "The difference is you played this course only twice a week while I played it twice a day, 365 days for seven years." Mentally he had teed off each day, playing not eighteen, but thirty-six holes without leaving his cell! Memory enabled him to "play" the eighteen holes, his game requiring four hours each time he went "around" the course.

It would be a tragedy if either the intellect or emotions developed at the expense of the other. The simple truth is that *both* are vital. Earlier in this century William James, the noted Harvard physician-psychologist, observed, "It is our attitude at the beginning of a difficult undertaking which, more than anything else, will determine its successful outcome."

·5·

Spirituality: Your Missing Link?

When writing to a syndicated column dealing with stress, readers correspond freely about the pathos in their lives, especially their heart-felt concerns. Some of the most difficult responses in answering column mail involve those letters where individuals have had to cope with the trauma of the death of a loved one, yet have no spiritual base for personal guidance. As the only being who does not find ultimate fulfillment in life on planet earth, man reaches out, attempting to bridge the chasm between this stage of life and whatever form awaits us next. Is it all vain hope, as Alexander Pope wrote?

> Hope springs eternal in the human breast:
> Man never is, but always to be, blest.

Or was the skeptic correct when he commented disparagingly on life?

> All that it is, is a hole in the ground
> And a scratch on a crumbling stone.

When we look about at the numerous signs of life's orderliness, doesn't it appear more rational to conclude with Emerson:

> All that I have seen teaches me to trust
> the Creator for all I have not seen.

Immediately there are those who argue, "But what about the religious fanatics?" We can only respond, "What *about* them?" It is possible to become a fanatic on any subject—religion included—but this doesn't negate the need for a spiritual base any more than abusing food negates the body's physical need for nourishment.

If one is to be a well-rounded and whole person, none of the four basic areas in life can be ignored. Each is as important as the other three, so that the physiological, sociological, psychological, and spiritual are of equal value. None is any more nor any less important than the other three.

The question may then arise: What purpose is served by attempting to meet man's spiritual needs? To begin with, man has his limitations, as all but the most egocentric would readily admit. When man has done everything within his power to change or correct a situation, he is faced with giving up or turning the matter over to a Source or Power greater than himself. Nowhere is this more readily seen than in adjusting to the shock following the unexpected death of a loved one.

There is no way anyone who has not experienced such a sudden loss can identify with those who have. This is not the time to state naively, "I know just how you feel," when indeed you have experienced no comparable loss. In coping with the trauma of the occasion we are left to ponder thoughts from those great writers and thinkers who drank deeply from the well of thought before us, as well as support from other sources which can help to salve our wounds. One perspective that has proven helpful to so many is "Meditation on Death," which comes to us anonymously from a book of meditations by Dr. Leslie R. Smith. In comparing death's passage to a ship's voyage, it reads:

Meditation on Death

I am standing upon the seashore; a ship at my side spreads her white sails to the morning breeze and starts for the blue ocean.

She is an object of beauty and strength, and I stand and watch her until—at length—she hangs like a speck of white cloud just where the sea and sky come down to mingle with each other.

Then someone at my side says, "There! She's gone." Gone where? Gone from my sight—that is all.

She is just as large in mast and hull and spar as she was when she left my side and just as able to bear her load of living freight to its place of destination.

Her diminished size is in me, not in her; and just at the moment when someone at my side says, "There! She's gone," there are other eyes watching her coming and other voices ready to take up the glad shout, "There she comes!"

And that is dying.

—Author Unknown

"Ah," but the cynic inquires, "what about the great thinkers? Haven't most of them been cynical regarding death?" Hardly! In fact, most of them have concluded that it is nearly impossible to conceive of life ending at the grave. Most of these same intellectuals would feel comfortable with the thoughts expressed in a letter by an early American patriot, one of the least-formally educated men in our history, Benjamin Franklin, who wrote a relative upon the death of his brother:

Philadelphia, Feb. 23, 1776

I condole with you. We have lost a dear and valuable relation. But it is the will of God and nature, that these mortal bodies be laid aside, when the soul is to enter real life. This is rather an embryo state, a preparation for living.

A man is not completely born until he is dead. Why then should we grieve, that a new child is born among the immortals, a new member added to their happy society? We are spirits. That bodies should be lent us, while they can afford us pleasure, assist us in acquiring knowledge, or in doing good to our fellow creatures, is a kind and benevolent act of God. When they become unfit for these purposes, and afford us pain instead of pleasure, instead of an aid become an encumbrance, and answer none of the intentions for which they were given, it is equally kind and benevolent, that a way is provided by which we may get rid of them. Death is that way. We ourselves, in some cases, prudently choose a partial death. A mangled painful limb, which cannot be restored, we willingly cut off. He who plucks out a tooth, parts with it freely, since the pain goes with it; and he, who quits the whole body, parts at once with all pains and possibilities of pains and diseases which it was liable to, or capable of making him suffer.

Our friend and we were invited abroad on a party of pleasure, which is to last forever. His chair was ready first, and he is gone before us. We could not all conveniently start together; and why should you and I be grieved by this, since we are soon to follow, and know where to find him?

Adieu,

B. Franklin

"But," the skeptic inquires, "is death the only subject where the spiritual process is applicable?" Of course not! A spiritual base adds an extra dimension to life, making us aware of an Ultimate Source far greater than man. Hence, man does not have the last word nor final answer when confronting life's trials. Before the disdainful "So what?" is heard, reflect on the role of the spiritual process played in the World War II Pacific Theatre episode involving Captain Eddie Rickenbacker, related by Lowell Thomas. Considered too old for uniform service in the forties, he took leave as head of Eastern Airlines to journey around the globe, reporting on the Allied air situation to world leaders. One day he was asked to take a message to General Douglas MacArthur, who was directing the Pacific fighting from New Guinea. With a crew of seven, Rickenbacker left Honolulu on October 21, 1942.

His plane failed to reach its first scheduled stop. For weeks he and his men floated around on three rafts tied together after having ditched their plane at sea. With the exception of four oranges, rations and water were lost on splashdown. Every other day one of these oranges was divided into eight small pieces. The men were scorched by the tropical sun during the day, and night brought bone-chilling breezes from the wind and flying spray. As sharks bumped against the rafts, it was left to Eddie, as leader of the pontoon, to revive sinking spirits. The days dragged on and the men began to reach the end of their endurance. When one died, Eddie taunted the others challenging them to stay alive. When they were finally rescued after floating for twenty-four days, one of the survivors pointing to Rickenbacker, exclaimed, "The only reason I didn't give up and die is that I wanted to live long enough to see that S.O.B. die first!" Eddie's ploy had worked!

Rickenbacker recognized the importance of discipline and scheduling in establishing a routine for the men aboard the three little rafts those long days and nights in the Pacific. Prayer meetings were held each day, beginning with the words from Psalm 139, "If I take the wings of the morning, and dwell in the uttermost parts of the sea, even there shall Thy hand lead me and Thy right hand shall hold me."

The spiritual process is a constant challenge to the intellect, stretching the mind, for as Dr. Ralph Sockman, minister of Christ Methodist Church in New York City for over forty years, once suggested, "The larger the island of knowledge, the longer the shoreline of wonder." However, the problem for many isn't one of disbelief, but rather of a belief that has never been nurtured to maturity. Somehow such people miss the wholeness of life, losing sight of life's ultimate challenge in their obsession with death. It was Cardinal Newman who grasped this problem so well when he advised, "Fear not that your life shall come to an end, but rather that it shall never have a beginning."

A spiritual base helps us become what we were meant to be. For each of us there is an ideal and a real. The ideal is who we might be; the real is who we have become with all our imperfections. If the ideal and the real were the same, we would have nothing to strive for, but if the difference between the ideal state and reality becomes too great, intense stress is likely. People become depressed, recognizing how far short they have fallen from their goals.

Development of a working code of ethics is the first order of priority in examining one's life in search of a healthy spiritual base. While some may experience the difficulty referred to by the late President Lyndon Baines Johnson when he said, "The difficulty is not in choosing right over wrong, but in knowing what is right," most of us do know what is right. It is *acting* upon what we know is right that is difficult. Temptations abound, even when we are making a concerted effort to choose right over wrong.

Certainly this was true for the Baptist fellow who had worked in a lumber yard for twenty years. During this time he had stolen enough lumber to build three houses. As he grew older, his conscience began to bother him so that he recognized a need to talk to someone about his misdeeds. Living in a small town he wasn't about to seek out his own Baptist preacher, so instead he went to the local Catholic priest. Entering the confessional booth, he knelt and said, "Father, I have sinned all these years by stealing enough lumber to build three houses," whereupon the priest said, "Son, arise and go in peace; your sins are forgiven." The penitent jumped to his feet and started out when the priest stopped him saying it wasn't quite so easy, that he would have to make penance. Forgetting for a moment that this wasn't one of his regular Catholic parishioners who would understand the word *Novena* (which means "constructing a new way of life"), the priest said, "You will also have to build a Novena." The fellow looked at him quizzically for a moment and then with his face breaking into a broad smile, commented, "Father, I really don't know what a Novena is—but if you can get the plans, I can get the lumber!"

Unfortunately the ethical code of too many of us is hardly any better. At the first temptation, we discard our ethics in favor of expediency, especially in answer to an immediate need. However, not only is the role we establish for ourselves important, but what about the impression we make on others? Is your ethical code one that makes you proud? Does it set before others examples that help them strengthen their lives, or does it encourage both you and others to chip away at the moral fiber of your lives?

Parents who take a teenager to a movie, claiming the child is only twelve years old so they can save on the price of admission are incurring a debt far greater than the few cents they saved. The example held out before the child is one of an ethic which operates according to the situation—in this case that a "little" cheating and lying are permissible. Yet, where is the logic in such teachings?

A friend described having visited a man whose son had been picked up that day for shoplifting at the local hardware store. The father was incredulous that his son would stoop to such a dishonest act. For nearly an hour he railed, citing numerous situations in which he had tried to set a good example before his boy. As my friend left, only then did he notice the shopping cart from the nearby grocery chain on the man's front porch, which he obviously used weekly to transport his groceries home. Was it the father's property? Had he just "borrowed" it? Wasn't he planning to return it to its rightful owner in due time? Regardless of the rationalization involved, what kind of an impression did this "borrowed" grocery cart make on the son? Ethics must be both *con*sistently and *per*sistently applied if they are to equip us with a strong spiritual base, preparing us to live at our best, while sending a message of equally positive motivating strength to those around us.

Of course, life is hardly so simple as to present *all* ethical dilemmas in stark contrasts of wrongs versus rights. There are gradations—which is precisely why people have to work at making moral decisions. Even when dealing with two rights, it isn't sufficient to arrive randomly at a decision;

rather, for your own sake and to strengthen your own spiritual base, you must weigh the alternatives before deciding.

For those who are as careful in meeting needs in this fourth area — the spiritual — as in the other three, the physiological, sociological, and psychological, the dividends are great. In the quietude of life, just before dropping off to sleep at night, or facing yourself in the mirror at the start of the day, how do you feel about yourself? Will you be glad five years hence for the decisions you make today? Will your sleep be the restful bliss of one who knows he has done his best to choose the "harder right over the easier wrong," an idea embodied in the Cadet Prayer at the United States Military Academy? A strong code of ethics is a guarantee of a clear conscience, and as the wag suggested, "A sleeping pill is a poor substitute for a clear conscience."

Memorization of the following lines may help you become more ethical in your daily living. It will assist you in becoming a person of greater integrity.

The Guy in the Glass*

When you get what you want in your struggle for self
And the world makes you "King" for a day,
Then go to the mirror and look at yourself
And see what that guy has to say.

For it isn't your father, or mother, or wife
Whose judgment upon you must pass;
The fellow whose verdict counts most in your life
Is the guy staring back from the glass.

He's the fellow to please — never mind all the rest,
For he's with you clear to the end.

And you've passed your most dangerous, difficult task
If the guy in the glass is your friend.

You may be like Jack Horner and "chisel" a plum
And think you're a wonderful guy,
But the man in the glass says you're only a bum
If you can't look him straight in the eye.

You can fool the whole world down the pathway
   of years
And get pats on the back as you pass,
But your final reward will be heartaches and tears
If you've cheated the guy in the glass.

                                    —*Dale Wimbrow*

*Reprinted by permission of Charisma Publications, Inc.

Shakespeare said it best, "To thine own self be true for then thou canst be false to no man." Being true to one's self is basic in developing life's greatest virtue, integrity. Just how important is integrity to successful living? It might just be the one ingredient that gives one person the edge over all competitors.

Life consists of very few total winners, with others cast as complete losers. Winners and losers are nearly always clustered together. Frequently there is little actual difference between the winner and other competitors, but what a difference the extra edge makes for the one who wins! In the 1981 running of the Kentucky Derby, the winner, Pleasant Colony, won more than $317,000 while Woodchopper, in second place, won only $28,000. Yet, the difference between Pleasant Colony and Woodchopper was less than half a length, or three feet!

In winning the 1981 World Series, the Dodgers didn't walk away with the pennant. Losing the first two games, they came from behind to edge the Yankees in the next four games, winning the Series. The difference between the two teams obviously wasn't great but the winning Dodgers were rewarded with $1,491,501.82, while the Yankees pocketed only $28,845.17. Differences in succeeding and *almost* succeeding are frequently minute, but as William James observed almost a century ago, "An unlearned carpenter of my acquaintance once said in my hearing: 'There is very little difference between one man and another; but what little there is, is very important!'" What a difference the *extra* ingredient—or edge makes!

You can heat water to 211 degrees, hot enough to sanitize dishes, to wash a load of clothes, or to make shaving easier. But when heated only one more degree steam is produced, a substance sufficient to run giant generators creating enough electricity to heat thousands of homes!

Often the difference between success and failure is also just a matter of degree. This is especially true in the working world. When you and another are considered for a promotion, is not comparable to night over day, but rather consists of two people fairly equal in what they have to offer the company. Eventually a choice is made, usually on minor points of distinction, which, when taken by themselves, do not seem so important, but which are vital in deciding who wins and who gets left by the wayside.

As a salesman (and which of us isn't involved in selling something?) when you lose a sale, is the other product or idea really superior to yours? Usually the answer is "No," but the item purchased or sales talk had a winning edge, however small, as judged by another.

Is there a winning edge in life that distinguishes the winners from the losers and, if so, how do we develop it? Is there a foolproof formula for success? Arthur Gordon, author of *A Touch of Wonder,* feels there is.

Gordon contends that college record, brains, and know-how—all are important, but the plus factor for success in life involves the magic characteristic of integrity. The word *integrity* means "wholeness"; this means that people of integrity don't think one thing and say another, nor do they believe in one thing only to do something else. For people with integrity there is an absence of inner warfare, releasing their energies to focus on external achievements. Gordon contends that integrity involves:

- living up to the best in yourself;
- developing a sense of honor, not just honesty;
- having a conscience *and* listening to it;
- having the courage of your convictions;
- being obedient to the unenforceable, that is, doing what is right not because if you don't others will know, but because *you* will know.

How can you become a person of integrity, acquiring that competitive edge which will make you a winner in your chosen field? First, practice total honesty in all things, especially the little, seemingly insignificant matters. Next, avoid the temptation to tell the small lie when it's inconvenient to tell the truth, and don't cheat even in small ways, for example, taking home office stationery or pens and pencils, though you know they won't be missed. Combined, these efforts form a mighty force that will sweep you along toward a victorious end. Integrity—the winner's edge—is not an attribute to be taken lightly!

"How does integrity apply to my personal life?" you may ask. You begin by avoiding harmful patterns. This requires emphasis on long-term rather than short-term needs gratification and presumes a certain maturity in decision-making in everyday life.

Nowhere does the need for integrity become more apparent than in interpersonal relationships, which are markedly influenced by the spirituality—or lack of it—within us. For example, how constructive are live-in arrangements between a man and a woman when no marital commitment has been made? A reader of the syndicated column, "Families Under Stress," wrote that for several months she had been dating a man she cared about who lived out of town, which led to the practice of spending alternate weekends at his place and then hers. When he made a passing comment about their "living in sin," she was left with intense anxiety, inquiring, "Could he view me as cheap?" The answer is "possibly but not probably," *provided* he doesn't subscribe to the outdated belief that morality within a relationship is the sole responsibility of the female. Obviously both partners are equally responsible.

However, rather than emphasizing what his statement suggests about his view of her, it would be more profitable to explore what it suggests about the way he views the existing relationship between the two of them. His reference to "living in sin" suggests that he is not totally pleased with their arrangement. Is this something he insisted upon earlier, yet now questions? Was she mainly responsible for the alternate weekend live-in arrangement plan, or did it "just happen"? Thinking back upon this development, it might be helpful to remember that *no* behavior just happens: all behavior has a cause.

Problems are numerous with the live-in arrangement. Of foremost concern is the lack of commitment. Each person knows the situation is temporary, one which can be nullified by either party simply by refusing to participate further. At least in marriage there has been a commitment made by each party, sanctioned by themselves, the church, the community, and the law. A live-in arrangement is weakened not only because of the lack of sanctions, but also by the perceptions this causes of the relationship, precisely that it is (1) not an ultimate commitment and (2) illicit in nature. To argue that you never know a person until you have lived with him or her is not a good reason to begin a live-in arrangement. In truth, you can spend a lifetime with someone and still not *really* know the person, due, if for no other reason, to the constant, continuing change occurring in all personalities.

Courtship is important in building a relationship. It provides an opportunity for the sheer joy of the chase, which either becomes so tempting a pursuit that both decide to end the chase and begin the real race of making their relationship work permanently, or one or both become disillusioned, ending the pursuit. A live-in arrangement — even temporary — nullifies the singular advantage of courtship with its extended time period in which two people get to know one another by interacting under many conditions. Just as the rising of yeast cannot be hastened in making rolls, so a developing relationship cannot be hurried. Honesty and openness must exist in any good relationship. We need to level with our partners when we are concerned. Each individual has an investment in this relationship, but consider: does a temporary live-in arrangement add to or detract from the joys each participant should be experiencing? Finally, if marriage is an ultimate goal, does such a live-in arrangement enhance or reduce the chances for marriage? Surely this is a question worthy of serious thought.

Arguments abound for other sexual arrangements which are at cross purposes with the traditional marriage commitment. One of these is mate-swapping with its supposed advantage of novelty and sexual attractiveness, including (1) an air of excitement from participating in socially unapproved behavior; (2) variety, which we are often told is "the spice of life"; (3) at least an occasional fleeting romantic feeling, and (4) a temporary respite from boredom. Yet, are these advantages or disadvantages? What we first perceive as advantages may soon be seen as disadvantages.

One such mate who wanted to continue mate-swapping, chided his spouse with, "Only the mature can handle these situations." Yet, is this logical when applied to the "advantages" mentioned above? Evidence to the contrary suggests:

(1) Excitement from indulging in illicit behavior is shortlived. There is no way this level of excitement can be maintained without escalating the variety of behavior or the numbers of people involved in swapping. When this pathological behavior occurs, it is evident that the individuals involved have lost their ability to distinguish between right and wrong.

(2) Variety is the spice of life, so we hear. Most males occasionally imagine it would be better if they could temporarily change sexual partners. Compared with known imperfections in marriage, it is impossible for one's mate to live up to the "spice" from a variety of imagined sexual partners. As we all know, fantasies of a "perfect relationship" seldom survive when exposed to the glare of reality, which is the real danger in shifting them from the realm of imagination.

(3) Romantic feelings are fun, but in this instance, would they be worth the price? Romanticism pales when compared with feelings of love that nurture in-depth relationships. Indeed, romanticism is an elementary stage of love. Only mature relationships move beyond this elementary, albeit powerful, feeling. When nothing of greater depth follows

romanticism, it is understandable that we feel cheapened and used by the experience.

(4) Finally, any temporary relief from boredom may result in problems far more damaging than the initial frustration.

The problem with making decisions and judgments in our personal lives and relationships with others is that our spirituality is based on a hodgepodge of beliefs that has been accumulated over the years. Some beliefs are valid while others need to be re-examined both for inherent logic as well as validity. Though it is impossible for us to possess qualifications necessary to pass moral judgment on another, we do use logic and pass judgments on lesser matters regularly. Every time we select one attorney over another we are passing our judgment on each, assigning one greater value than the other. Whenever we purchase an automobile, the product is judged more suitable for our needs than those not chosen. This is the case with every decision made, provided alternate products or services are available. Grocery store layouts compete for the shopper's eye, with an array of goods forcing the customer to make dozens of choices before approaching the check-out counter. Nor are such judgments limited to the commercial world. Our group of friends is the result of judgments and selections we have made.

In spite of passing judgments daily, we should avoid emphasizing the failures or shortcomings of another. Not only does this practice injure another, but it speaks poorly of the one criticizing. It also tends to make us chronic complainers who recognize all of life's failures and too few of its successes. This negative approach soon affects all of life, making failure more likely than success. Finally, emphasizing what is wrong in others lessens our ability to note the good in them. There is no quicker way to become an undesirable acquaintance—one who will be avoided at every opportunity—than to put emphasis on the negative. If by habit we have begun to look first for the negative, we should work to reverse this practice. If we speak ill of another because of jealousy, we need to remind ourselves that the success field is open for other front-runners. In any event, life's winners are too busy to waste time criticizing others.

The role we assume in directing and routing those thoughts which enter our minds is essential. In the computer industry, when biased statistics are fed into the computer, it is said, "Garbage in, garbage out." The meaning is clear: if contaminated data are fed a program, any statistical analysis is worthless. Further, if such an analysis is used to implement programs, these are destined to fail because they are based on false data. Similarly, if we are not careful about what is fed into our minds, our streams of conscious thought will be adversely affected. Simply put, you can think your way to failure and unhappiness, true, but you can also think your way to success and happiness. It was Ralph Waldo Emerson, respected as the "Sage of Concord," who once declared, "A man is what he thinks about all day long."

Certainly this is true in the spiritual realm where cause and effect are as absolute in the hidden recesses of thought as in the material world. You can raise yourself up or tear yourself down simply by your thoughts, and although you cannot control thoughts coming to your mind, you are charged with the role of standing sentinel at the mind's door, guarding the gateway of entry. For as John Churton Collins observed:

> We are no more responsible for the evil thoughts that pass through our minds than a scarecrow for the birds which fly over the seedplot he has to guard. The sole responsibility in each case is to prevent them from settling.

Thus, you are responsible for thoughts entering and *remaining* in the conscious stream, which is the foundation upon which character is built.

Since spirituality is so important, the question then arises—Just how important is church attendance to the development of the spiritual process? To be spiritual or religious, must one attend church?

It is possible to be deeply religious and yet not involved in church. Further, we can participate in worship in virtually any setting; hence, we can worship regularly though never attending a formal service. However, note that the emphasis is placed on what is *possible*. It is *possible* to worship on the golf course, driving an automobile, or out on a boat, though the inherent distractions in these activities are hardly conducive to worship. Still, there are many who find strength in quietly and silently meditating in many diverse settings.

What then about spiritual growth? Can one continue to grow spiritually without attending church? The answer again is, "Yes, it is possible," probably about as possible as:

> a student who will not go to school;
> a citizen who will not pay taxes or vote;
> a salesman without customers;
> a business man on a deserted island;
> an author without readers;
> an instrumentalist without an orchestra;
> a scientist who does not share his findings;
> a player without a team.

So we end this chapter where we started, i.e., to be a whole person, needs must be met in each of the four primary areas—the physiological, sociological, psychological, and spiritual. Growth in these areas is never-ending. Ask yourself, "What have I done today to strengthen the spiritual process in my own life as I continue on the journey toward becoming a whole person?"

Stress Inventory VII
Your Spiritual Quotient

Answer each of the following True or False as it applies to you.

True False

( )   ( )   1. I regularly withdraw from my usual hectic pace to refresh and restore the mind.

( )   ( )   2. The spiritual process in my life receives as much attention as the other three aspects, i.e., the physiological, sociological, or psychological.

( )   ( )   3. I feel relatively comfortable when considering and discussing the subject of death with others.

( )   ( )   4. I am satisfied with the gap between the "ideal" and the "real" in my life, or the difference between the one I am and the one I can become.

( )   ( )   5. Most of the time I feel good about the way I have treated myself and others.

( )   ( )   6. Anxieties over my day's activities seldom cause me to lose sleep at night.

( )   ( )   7. A sense of honor is as important to me as honesty.

( )   ( )   8.   Even when I know I won't get caught, I usually choose the "harder right over the easier wrong."

( )   ( )   9.   When a clerk makes a mistake giving me too much change, I am as likely to call it to his attention as when the error favors the store.

( )   ( )   10.   I believe regular church attendance is important to help me develop a spiritual life.

To score, count the number of checks in the True column. A score of 8 or more indicates you probably pay adequate attention to the development of your spiritual life. A score of 5 to 7 indicates an average amount of attention is focused on this area. Fewer than 5 indicates a need for improvement if you are to become a truly whole and well-balanced person.

Part Two

Coping with Stress

·6·

Stress Starts at Home

The director of a psychiatric evaluation center, Alfred Vent, once remarked, "Having completed ten years of work with a variety of corporate executives, we have reached a firm finding: *job stress is always family based!*"

There is no question that stress exacts a toll, both in the home and on the job. Most of us probably cope with job-related stress primarily the way we learned to handle stress in our homes during our formative years. This chapter will examine what we learned about stress as children and how, as adults, we can be most successful in the potentially stressful relationships which are part of what we call home: parenting, marriage itself, two-paycheck marriages, divorce, and living single.

To begin with, what does the family teach? Of course there are extreme cases, such as the recent one where authorities removed eight-and nine-year-old children from an extended family in which they were being taught how to steal, cheat, and lie. But the unusual aside, what is being taught about family life in the more typical family setting?

Dr. Robert Coles, writing on "Our Self-Centered Children—Heirs of the Me Decade," in the *U.S. News and World Report,* notes:

> ...Many children drug themselves, knock themselves out with liquor, or run away. They are running from neglect and parental abuse by parents so wrapped up in their own personal trajectories that they don't offer their children some moral and spiritual vision to hold on to and to try to live up to. Families don't discuss the meaning of life but rather are concerned with what we can get today and tomorrow.

From this statement then the question arises regarding family stress—Are we as parents so concerned with our own personal interests that the welfare of our children is only incidental or secondary at best?

Sometimes parents err in a different direction, putting too much emphasis on their parental rather than their marital roles. Not only does the marriage suffer, but the children as well. I have long been of the opinion that "poor mates do not make good parents."

Our children are taught best by examples they observe in the home. Where parents seldom treat one another kindly or even neglect to show each other everyday courtesies, children's minds record these images for later recall. Homes tend to procreate themselves, which should not come as a surprise in that it is in the home where most teaching takes place, especially in the early, impressionable years for the child.

Others might point to change as the culprit which causes the family excessive trauma. Certainly change—which is neither bad nor good necessarily—can represent a hodgepodge of blessings and curses for any family. As an example, when we rail out against the inevitable change affecting modern

90

family life, not many of us would opt for a return to what life was really like in the "good old days." There was a time when fewer than 50 percent of us completed high school and finding females on college campuses was almost as rare as discovering them in one of the professions. However, today's medical advances not only prolong life, but enhance its quality for many who once would have viewed death as a merciful way to be free of pain.

When the train was invented, someone remarked how wonderful it was, for now missionaries could fan out over the entire continent in record time to perform their good deeds. A realist remarked, "Yes, but this same change also provides thieves with increased opportunities for their misdeeds." Similarly, change has produced both desirable and undesirable results for the American family in recent decades.

Our high divorce rate is accompanied by a high remarriage rate. While a high divorce rate is hardly desirable, there is comfort in recognizing that an increasing number of the divorced opt for remarriage. Obviously family life is attractive, in fact so attractive that even those who have had less than desirable previous experiences choose to try again by forming new family units.

Further, courts are no longer arbitrarily excluding fathers from being awarded child custody. Fathers are increasingly given equal consideration with mothers before custody is granted. This change is especially constructive where the father is the better qualified of the two parents to meet the child's needs. Granting custody to the male in the past was usually dismissed out of hand unless the mother was shown to be grossly unfit. On the other hand, neither men or women continue to be burdened with the myth of the divine right of male dominance. This has brought about equality in

91

many marital relationships which would have been unthinkable only fifty years ago.

When couples separate today, wives receive fairer legal settlements than in the past. Though much is still left to be desired, change has produced more equity between the battling spouses in recent years. Many states are still far from the best solution, i.e., awarding spouses half of everything accumulated by the two of them since marrying, but fortunately, this trend is increasing.

Adjusting and coping with all of these changes, each of which affects the family, is a challenge for everyone. Yet, rather than viewing change as the enemy, we need to examine it for any inherent benefits. Strange though it may seem at first glance, separation and divorce are two of those changes with mixed benefits and liabilities, depending upon the circumstance and perspective.

Today we are aware that an increasing number of couples who have been married for twenty or more years are separating and divorcing. These separations are traumatic, especially if the wife has not worked outside the home in years and doesn't have skills that are marketable in the changing workplace. Also, when parents convince themselves their decision to divorce will be more readily acceptable now that the children are grown, they are often faced with a rude awakening. Many of these adult children are left bewildered by their parents' separations.

Obviously we are living longer today with greater life expectancies, which in turn leads to increased demands on marriage. Not long ago, once parents entered the empty-nest stage, with all children launched from the home, not many years passed before death claimed one or both of them. With today's average forty-five-year-old expecting to live to age seventy-five, mates are less willing to devote an additional thirty years to a marriage they regard as hopeless.

Growing apart over the years is probably the chief reason for much of the soaring divorce rate occurring after twenty years of marriage. The scenario is recognized by all marriage counselors: the husband devoted more of himself to his job as the years passed, while the wife lost herself in rearing the children. Dissatisfactions were never discussed, only privately milked for all they were worth: he, when away on a business trip with ample time to reflect; or she when at home with endless hours alone where her mind could dwell on life's inequities. Eventually they found they really shared nothing, had little in common, with too many negatives for them simply to pick up and build their marriage anew. When denial has been practiced so diligently that one of the partners cannot imagine life apart from the other, separation sets the stage for extreme depression or even potential thoughts of suicide. Yet, this need not be the end-result of those who divorce late in life.

Change always produces opportunity, if only we will search for it. One man, divorced late in life, was able to change from a career he had disliked for many years and enter a vocation where, he reports, "For the first time in my life I feel I am making a contribution that counts." While married, both partners had put such emphasis on their possessions that he had never felt he could give up his lucrative salary.

A woman, finding herself without marital bonds after twenty-four years, decided to return to school. Her undergraduate degree was earned more than a quarter of a century earlier, but she returned to graduate school, receiving her M.B.A. Today, she is personnel manager for a small manufacturing company and feeling better than she has in years. She reports: "For the first time in my life, I feel in control."

What about remarriage for those divorcing *late* in life? Is there hope for a second union? In spite of the seeming obstacles, middle-aged couples are continuing to remarry following divorce. There are second marriages for five of every six men and three of every four women aged fifty to seventy-five whose first unions ended in divorce, according to the United States Census Bureau. Though this is not offered as an argument in favor of divorce and remarriage, it is offered as a note of hope that even in some of life's most difficult changes, stress needn't necessarily lead to distress.

Even in younger marriages, studies report that children will fare better in single-parent homes where there is an absence of dissension as opposed to an intact home where the climate is usually acrimonious. Obviously the preferable home is an intact one, in spite of its imperfections, where children learn to interact with members of the opposite sex by observing and participating in the love and consideration their parents show one another. However, if the home environment isn't healthy for the emotional growth and development of the child, just hanging on to an intact family setting regardless of the quality of family life can cause a great amount of distress.

Julie List in *The Day the Loving Stopped* wrote about divorce from her perspective as a nine-year-old, when her parents decided to call it quits. Though torn and troubled by the divorce, she later wrote, "Children, they say,...bounce back. I agree—children are terrific survivors." Her advice for parents who have young children and are considering divorce is to take care to explain to each child that the divorce isn't the child's fault. Just as importantly, it is crucial for the child to know it's all right to love both parents, regardless of who has custody.

Another helpful point is to avoid maligning the divorced spouse. It is detrimental to children to use them to convey negative or angry feelings to the other parent. Also, divorced parents must be careful to avoid forcing the children to make decisions for which they are ill-equipped. Young children should not have to choose which parent they will spend the holidays with when it is obvious the children would rather be with both. It is up to the parents to work out some schedule that each of them can accept.

Because children get attached so easily, divorced parents should be very careful about introducing another parental figure into the child's life. Where divorced parents remarry only to divorce fairly soon the second time, the child may be left bewildered, feeling deserted again. In spite of all the difficulties inherent in divorce for the young child, Julie List concludes, "My parents' divorce has made me wary and frightened of the decay of love. And yet...I believe in marriage. I now believe that lifetime intimacy is a risk worth taking."

Of course, marriage is a risk for both partners, because there is no guarantee that the relationship will work, be satisfying, and permanent. The risk factor is even greater today with the increase in infidelity, both sexual and emotional. Unfortunately, sexual infidelity in marriage is on the increase for both males and females. Many factors are cited as causing this increase, but some of the more basic reasons are often overlooked. Since it is still the husband who is more likely to seek sexual liaisons outside the marriage, what causes these men to stray, especially when their homes seem relatively attractive, even to many of them? Their motives differ. For instance, some men never move beyond a sexual adversary role. That is, women are objects to be conquered, not persons to be loved. Sexual conquests prove they still have the ability to attract and entice, feeding their egos each time they are successful. For these men, the sex act is secondary; rather, sexual activity is simply the "playing field" where they repeatedly prove their worth. A basic insecurity usually can be noted in these men.

Others substitute sexual activity for affection. Sex for these men is a habit, not entirely different from the habit of the drug addict. The "fix" sought by the philandering husband is reassurance that he is loved. He never progresses to a point of recognizing that sexual activity is a poor substitute for love, or even affection. Consequently, after each encounter he is left with the same need that drove him into the relationship just completed. This obsession centers on numbers, with his thinking that more sexual involvements will surely be the answer. However, this behavior is self-defeating, for such a person never learns that love is something to be built, not tested. Frustration is a hallmark of one driven with this obsession.

Then there is the male who argues that he is bored at home, that nothing new ever happens in his marriage. Rather than recognizing boredom as a trap victimizing both partners, he sees it as affecting only him. Self-centered, these males usually expect to be entertained in a relationship, seldom realizing that they, too, are responsible for any ensuing boredom. Couples need to work together in relationships to make certain that sameness doesn't create boredom. Unique approaches to sex within the marriage would be far more satisfying in the long run than sexual encounters with several different partners. However, such insight is usually not present in these men.

It is difficult for mates who feel they no longer occupy the primary position in their spouses' lives to acknowledge other persons or interests have usurped what was once their exclusive domain. This comes from a variety of causes, but the biggest factor is time. As other interests or exposure to people in the working world take up more time, it is easy to develop a dependency pattern outside the marriage, usually to the detriment of the marital relationship.

Communication and sharing are important in any marriage. If your marriage is not as satisfying as you had hoped, examine Stress Inventory VIII for a brief marital checkup. This will help make you aware of areas where changes are needed for your relationship to become more fulfilling and to channel any stress into eustress, with positive results for you and your mate.

Stress Inventory VIII
Level of Marital Satisfaction

Answer each of the following items True or False as you assess your marriage at present:

True False

(.) ( ) 1. My marriage is as fulfilling as I had expected.

( ) (-) 2. The times I am glad I am married far outnumber those when I wish I were still single.

(-) ( ) 3. My mate is generally respectful of my feelings.

(-) ( ) 4. I am usually considerate of my mate's desires.

(-) ( ) 5. Most of my daydreams and fantasies involve my mate in a complimentary manner.

(-) ( ) 6. When I have a free evening, I prefer spending it with my mate.

(-) ( ) 7. Both of us are increasingly finding areas of agreement the longer we are married.

( )   (✓)   8.   Our philosophies on handling money, relating to in-laws, and socializing with friends are similar.

(✓)   ( )   9.   Each of us has individual friends, as well as couple friends both of us enjoy.

(✓)   ( )   10.   I feel assured that I can trust my mate with *any* secret, knowing my trust would never be betrayed.

Key: Eight or more True answers indicates a strong, healthy marriage.

Five to seven True answers suggest a basically healthy marriage, but one that could benefit from working together in areas answered in the negative.

Four or fewer True answers place a marriage in a category of possible jeopardy. Help would probably be beneficial from some professional affiliated with the American Association of Marriage and Family Therapists, an organization of professionals who by their training are especially equipped to help couples work through marital and family problems.

Some people view divorce as the worst of life's outcomes, as we have already observed. There are those now divorced who would agree. One writer to the syndicated column, "Families Under Stress," wrote:

> After 24 years of what many of our friends considered a "perfect" marriage, we divorced last year. If I had it to do over, I wouldn't have agreed to divorce. Our marriage wasn't all that happy, but my life was far better then than now. My advice to those thinking of divorce is "Don't"—unless the relationship is unbearable. I wish I had received this advice before last year. It would definitely have made a difference for me.

The case for weighing the situation very carefully before filing for divorce is stated most eloquently here. This is especially applicable to long marriages, where individuals have invested over half their lives with each other. To break off and start life anew at this point is not unlike experiencing the death of a mate. Washington psychiatrist Dr. Barton Kraff says, "Divorce is like the death of the family. Then in mid- or late-life they must start anew. People tend to underestimate the ramifications. They can be enormous."

Often divorce for the mature couple is devastating, maybe more so for the female than for the male. Unfortunately for many of these women, no preparations were ever made for alternatives to marriage. Had their mates died, society may have extended more of a helping hand than is usually the case following divorce. Consequently, many divorced women feel the unhappily married state was far preferable to that of being unhappily divorced. Marriage counselors report that today more males are concurring.

Divorce is usually not what either partner had anticipated. Being too idealistic about the past and the future is one of the major reasons. Many people remember far greater happiness in their former marriages than actually existed. Memory often dulls the recall of the negative, presenting the impossible task of comparing the past with the present. This must be remembered when looking back wistfully on a former marriage. At the same time, it is easy for those who are unhappily married to look ahead, idealizing the future. Unrealistic post-marital expectations are responsible for much personal unhappiness.

Divorce is society's way of providing a "safety net" for couples who feel they can no longer stay married. If a marriage is destroying one or both parties, divorce provides an "out." No one should feel constrained to remain in an unhealthy relationship which produces nothing but heartaches. Those who believe there is nothing worse than divorce might be reminded that there is one state far worse than divorce: *a dismal marriage where there is no hope of improvement.* Yet, the point is well taken that some divorced persons might have evaluated the divorce option differently had they known earlier what they learned later.

For couples who have considered divorce even fleetingly, there are warning signals to watch for when a relationship needs help. If you are routinely unhappy to see your spouse, or wish he or she weren't coming home at night, you might need professional help. Similarly, if either mate constantly slights the other, leading to personal or public embarrassment, help is needed. When you find that you are sexually aroused only by others and never by your mate, then marriage counseling or individual therapy is advisable.

Of course all family stress isn't confined to nuclear or primary family relationships. Often our family stress expands to include the extended family. One example of this kind of stress is when we feel disappointed following a family reunion. For some people the letdown is so devastating that they begin to question the value of families getting together, even on special occasions. What we overlook is that our expectations at family reunions may be unrealistically high, setting the stage for disappointment. Usually family members have been separated long enough to become nostalgic about each other, forgetting obnoxious personality quirks, remembering only the good times. Another problem is trying to compress too much into too little time. We try to catch up for everything that has happened since we last met, which becomes fatiguing.

Most family reunions are probably neither innately bad nor good. They are about what we make them, beginning with our expectations prior to the event. Quite often expectations are too high when parents anticipate a child's homecoming after a first real step away from the family. There is never a homecoming equal to this one. However, the reality faced by many young people—whether they are in college coming back that first weekend or in the armed forces returning from basic training—is that they feel an emotional separation poignantly expressed by Thomas Wolfe as the theme and title of his book, *You Can't Go Home Again.*

Some of the stress in our homes comes from invalid or unrealistic expectations about different roles in the family. For example, in the past many people believed that for a woman to be a good mother she must remain in the home regardless of the ages of her children. Today it seems that most would agree that a mother's place is in the home *when she has preschoolers.* However, even in these instances, unless the mother wants to be in the home full-time, young children would probably reap greater benefits from a home environment where the mother was happier and presumably better equipped to fulfill her mothering role for fewer hours each day if she worked outside the home. Note that the issue isn't one of working versus not working, for many full-time mothers work as hard as any woman employed outside the home.

Sometimes relatives and other well-meaning adults help foster guilt in working mothers. However, we must avoid using the working mother as a scapegoat for society's ills. Juvenile crime, teenage pregnancy, truancy, drugs, and other problems faced by youth would not be substantially reduced just by mothers staying home. There is little evidence that homes are not run as well, or that the families where mothers have gone outside to work are on a track similar to freight trains racing downhill toward the pits of Dante's Inferno!

Working mothers of school-age children are only away from the house for approximately two hours each day when their children are home in need of after-school supervision; this care can be provided as well by another responsible adult. Children aren't harmed because they are with an adult other than their mothers for two additional hours each day.

Loved ones are sometimes jealous of the options now open to women. Males can be threatened by the prospect of females earning their own money, thereby becoming less dependent on them. Some wives whose husbands feel this may choose to remain in the home full-time. No one should put down this life style, for individual preference is what's important.

In many homes it is necessary for both the husband and wife to work. As more women continue to enter the working world away from home—and there is no reason to think this trend which started in World War II will subside—more attention needs focusing on the gap between pay for males and females doing similar work. For instance, in 1971, women earned 63 cents for every dollar men earned; today it's 59 cents. Although some of this difference may be based on the number of males who are better prepared for the work world, few would argue that financial discrimination no longer exists. In fact, this issue causes more stress and adds more fuel to the battle of the sexes, both in and outside the home, than any other single issue. Further, the Woman's Bureau of the U.S. Department of Labor reports that women earn less than men even when they have more education. The median income in 1981 for fully employed women high school graduates (with no college) was $11,537. The median for men who had not even completed elementary school was $11,753. Women with four years of college had a median income of $15,143, while men with only a high school diploma earned a median income of $19,469.

In answer to the myth that most working women don't need money as do men, the majority of women work *because* of economic need. Almost two-thirds of the women in the labor force in 1982 were single, widowed, divorced, separated, or had husbands earning less than $15,000, according to the Women's Bureau (*20 Facts on Women Workers,* 1982). Frequently it is the working mother whose earnings help the family move substantially above the poverty line. This is hardly news to today's parents, who are well aware that raising a child now costs an average middle-income American family $85,000, according to the Population Reference Bureau. This is the actual expense of rearing a child from birth, through eighteen years under the parental roof, followed by four years at a public university. Even for low-income families, the total cost of having and raising a child was estimated at $58,000.

In a 1981 updating of an earlier study on inflation for the Urban Institute, Thomas J. Espenshade, after adjusting his figures, concluded that the total economic cost confronting

American families in 1980 for child rearing varied "from slightly more than $100,000 at the low-income level to nearly $140,000 for middle-income families." Working mothers are apparently here to stay, which needn't cause distress in families where care is taken to make adequate adjustments. Indeed, "Families at Work: Strengths and Strains," a study of a cross population in the United States sponsored by General Mills, Inc., concluded that the majority of women want to, and will continue to, work outside the home — marriage and child-rearing responsibilities notwithstanding.

Another form of stress in the home occurs when people have unrealistic expectations about their own parenting. For example, parents may experience guilt when their young get into trouble. Yet, in such instances we, as parents, need to adjust our thinking, first, because we attempt to measure our efforts against those of a perfect parent, and second, because ultimately no one is responsible for the behavior of another. As conscientious parents we are constantly aware of our mistakes. However, if we can look back over our parenting years and honestly conclude, "I did my best — most of the time," we can ask no more. To wish we had done a better job is to compare our actual parenting role with an ideal, and the ideal parent is nonexistent. Perfection in human behavior has no place in any stage of development.

Another consideration involves children's responsibility for their own decisions. As they grow, children increasingly control their decision-making. By the time they reach their mid-teens, parents can advise and restrict, but basically the children make up their own minds. Teenagers spend most of their hours away from home, where they must continually exercise their own judgment. Hopefully, such teens have been reared in a home where solid values have been taught and will rely on these in making decisions, but there is no guarantee that this will be the case.

Parenting always involves stress. Hopefully, we can be as effective as we'd like to be. The following, Stress Inventory IX, offers some checkpoints for positive parenting.

Stress Inventory IX
Effective Parenting

Check each of the following statements which applies to you as a parent. Do you recall incidents with your children when:

_____ You treated them as if they had already become what you wanted them to be.

_____ Following at least one of their failures you refused to say, "I told you it wouldn't work!"

_____ You put aside your newspaper or favorite TV program to study and admire something they had made.

_____ You set aside time just for them, listening to whatever it was they had to tell you.

_____ In their presence you and your mate apologized to each other early in the day, erasing the day's bad start.

_____ You took that extra time to help them work through their feelings following defeat, helping them realize there's still something good to be said, even when they aren't the winners.

If these answers are unsatisfactory, regardless of the age of your child, you should seriously consider whether your emphasis is positive or negative and take corrective action where necessary.

Parents everywhere need to be careful of the type of teaching which occurs in the home. An age-old problem is that we teach in the negative. For instance, we say to the young child about to cross the street, "Watch out so you don't get run over." On other occasions we say, "Be careful so you don't get hurt." Both are examples of negative teaching. Children learn better and more effectively when the emphasis is on what they *should* do, not what they shouldn't do. For example, when teaching youngsters to drive, they are taught how to shift gears correctly and to steer the car in a straight path on their side of the road; they are not shown how gears can be stripped or given a lesson in driving on both sides of the centered double yellow line! The best learning occurs by imitating a good model, rather than being told what we can't or shouldn't do. As parents, we should avoid instructing by means of the "reverse of an idea," as Warren Spahn would agree.

Warren Spahn was a pitcher for the Milwaukee Braves. When the Braves faced the New York Yankees in the last game of the World Series several years ago, Spahn was on the mound. With Yankee players on all bases in the top of the ninth inning, Spahn had already struck out two men; the call on the third batter was three balls and two strikes. At that moment the Brave's manager walked onto the field. Approaching Spahn at the mound he said, "Whatever you do, don't give this man a high outside pitch." As Spahn prepared to deliver his next pitch, he thought repeatedly, "No high outside pitch, no high outside pitch." He wound up to make his most crucial throw—reflecting one last time on the manager's warning of no high outside pitch—but too late, he had let loose of the ball and immediately realized he had thrown precisely what he had been warned not to throw: a high outside pitch! The batter hit the ball out of the stadium, bringing in four runs and the Yankees won the pennant! Why had the Braves lost? Because the reverse of an idea had been taught. Ever since, Spahn has asked incredulously, "Why would *anyone* try to teach *anything* using the reverse of an idea?"

We must positively reinforce what we want our children to learn. For instance, we must teach them to be responsible with money so that they are well-trained to handle and manage money successfully when they become adults. Many children fully understand how to spend money but have little understanding of saving or investing. Acquiring good financial habits before leaving home is the *best* predictor of future fiscal responsibility.

To instruct your child in money management, a good first step is to establish a savings account of however modest proportions which can be added to periodically and later continue to grow from the child's own contributions. Also the child should be taught to set aside one portion of the earnings, 10 percent for example, to help others, with a second portion, perhaps another 10 percent, placed in savings. Anyone who follows this suggested plan as a child will have good financial habits as an adult.

Children should also be reared in a home where there are reasonable demands and responsibilities placed upon them. No child or adult should expect to live in a home without contributing to the well-being of the family unit. Since every family member receives from the group, each must make some contribution in return, including the very young. While it is fine to grant a young child an allowance, a formal connection should not be made between the allowance and doing specific chores. Then the child may assume that he can forego the chores in exchange for giving up the allowance. In addition, a child shouldn't expect payment for every service rendered. Children will profit best by learning that often the greatest satisfaction comes when one gives to another with no expectation of a return.

It is often difficult to know what to do as parents. However, there are some obvious things which we should *not* do, such as:

1. *Start at infancy giving the children whatever they want.* This assures them that caring for themselves is not their responsibility. Rather, they will grow up with the mistaken notion that the world owes them a living!

2. *Laugh at any profanity they utter.* Such children will see that these cute phrases get attention. The effect will be to encourage undesirable behaviors for attention-getting purposes, setting a dangerous precedent.

3. *Never, never, never use the word "wrong" around them.* Not only may this harm their emotional development, but now they can grow up convinced that whatever they do is right. Any development of their consciences should be left entirely to chance.

4. *Make certain they are never given any spiritual training.* Everyone knows that religion should never be forced on children. There will be plenty of time for them to decide for themselves when they get older.

5. *Let them read any material they can get their hands on.* Naturally we want to safeguard their physical health, but let their minds feed on whatever they can find. After all, what is fed the mind isn't nearly as important as what is fed the body.

6. *Always pick up after them.* By doing everything for them now, they will expect the same treatment when they leave home—especially upon marrying. A future spouse will just *love* us for the job we have done!

7. *Quarrel frequently in front of them.* It's not enough that they recognize our home isn't perfect. They should hear the

names we call each other when we're *really* mad. Later they won't be quite so shocked when the home breaks up.

8. *Give them all the spending money they want.* Don't encourage them to earn any of their own. After all, there's plenty of time for that later, and none of us wants our children to have things as tough as we did.

9. *Whenever a disagreement arises between our children and someone in authority, take the children's side.* Adults don't understand children, especially their own. And everyone knows children need protection, even when they're in the wrong.

10. *In late teens when the adolescent gets in real trouble, we'll simply shake our heads saying, "We never could do anything with that child."* The thought that we never gave parenting our best effort will be totally lost on us. After all, that would be a depressing admission of failure.

To reduce stress for the future parents should go back and carefully *reverse* each of these statements above. Remember: good parenting involves instilling discipline and responsibility, which helps the child make a successful transition from childhood to responsible adulthood.

While stress is present in marriages and families, it is also found in single life. Some singles feel that all their problems would be solved if only they were married. These individuals need to be reminded that people are about as happy in marriage as they were previously. *Marriage does not cause but can result in happiness.* Far from being free of problems, marriage simply requires an exchange of one set of problems for another. Where the single person fights loneliness, the spouse must sacrifice previously free time to work at building a marital relationship. The single person may feel there is never anyone special to do certain things with, though married partners occasionally will long for freedom to act on their own. While singles don't have a ready-made family setting available for the occasional festive holidays, there are many times when the young mother or father secretly desires a return to the "good old days," free of formula-mixing, sleepless nights holding a crying baby, or cajoling older children to be more responsible with their studies.

It is not being single or married that necessarily produces satisfaction; rather, it is the attitude of the individual—single or married—which is the primary cause of happiness or unhappiness. Failure to recognize this is due to what is called in psychological jargon the "halo effect," which occurs when we see only the positive in a situation, remaining oblivious to the negative.

The halo effect comes about when a person or situation is seen through rose-colored glasses. Can you recall the best family or most well-adjusted individual you have ever known? Everything seemed perfect, or as nearly perfect as possible. Compared with your own life, another's may have seemed so much better, but then you are intimately acquainted with your own failures and successes. However, with the other, only the successes are readily perceived. Recognizing only the good in another's life style does not make that life style preferable to yours. In reality, yours may be more desirable, if only you knew the whole truth about the other's. It is with the halo effect that most singles view marriage and, conversely, the way many married people see being single. However, when all is said and done, marriage remains a goal sought by most of us, especially in the United States where 95 percent of the population marries at least once. Certainly marriage has much to commend it; its chief asset is companionship. Still, life can be fulfilling and worthwhile in *either* the single or marital state.

In chapters seven and eight, the importance of helping employers and employees cope with stress in the home will be emphasized, for workers who are coping satisfactorily with stress in the home will be far better equipped to handle the inevitable stress on the job. As you review this chapter, hopefully it will seem possible that with a few changes, most of us *can* cope more adequately with stress at home *and* on the job. Indeed, stress that becomes eustress—rather than distress—is a welcome gift in anyone's life. So may it be in yours!

·7·

Unique to Employers

Leo Rosten in his book, *The Power of Positive Nonsense,* reported, "The enormous profits our corporations make—even after taxes—is a scandal!" This kind of statement by itself is enough to cause executives stress, especially when, as Rosten points out, such a belief exists in spite of evidence to the contrary. As an example he cites a study by Opinion Research Corporation where people were asked to estimate how much profit American oil companies made after taxes. A majority of respondents guessed 43 percent or forty-three cents for each dollar of sales while the actual profit for Mobil Oil during the year studied was less than four cents per dollar earned after taxes.

These same people estimated that the average automobile manufacturer made a profit of thirty-seven cents, when in fact only slightly over five cents per dollar was earned after taxes. This worry over a company's public image is just one of the many stresses unique to employers who are responsible generally to a board of directors, employees, and the public they serve. Is it any wonder that enlightened corporations are insisting that their leadership take regularly scheduled vacations? Every employer needs a break from the harassment accompanying the running of a large or small business.

Henry C. Goodrich, president of Inland Container Corporation, recognized that the many demands on executives have a direct influence on their relationships with their employees. He believed humor to be important in creating a compatible, happy staff. "It's a fundamental principle," he said, "that if you do something you enjoy, you'll be a better employee and a better employer." Although a sense of humor, tolerance, understanding, and ability to make decisions might be viewed as important employer traits to cultivate, are there other specifics that characterize the modern successful executive? According to Mr. Herbert T. Mines, chairman of Business Careers, Inc., the answer is a resounding, "Yes!" Previously, an executive in personnel and industrial relations for sixteen years with Macy's in New York and Nieman Marcus in Dallas, Mr. Mines was asked what it takes to get to the top in a big company today and stay there. He listed five traits as characterizing successful executives:

1. Singleness of purpose—the most important.
2. Consistent record of doing well in previous jobs.
3. Willingness to devote enormous time and energy to reach the goals set for self.
4. Emotional commitment to do well; getting along with colleagues and subordinates.
5. Happy marriage and stable home life.

This last point, incidentally, runs counter to popular belief about business executives. However, the individual who doesn't have support and sympathy from an understanding spouse is at a disadvantage in today's competitive business world.

Are you a successful executive or employer? How would your peers rate your success, or, just as revealing, how would those working for you rate you as an employer? Take a moment to rate yourself on Stress Inventory X.

Stress Inventory X
Assessing Successful Executive Traits

In the following inventory, first answer questions from your perspective, then as your superiors might rate you, and finally how your subordinates might respond if asked to rate you. Use the rating: 5 Always, 4 Usually, 3 Occasionally, 2 Seldom, 1 Never.

Your Assessment	Superiors' Assessment	Subordinates' Assessment		
( )	( )	( )	1.	Completes a job once it's begun.
( )	( )	( )	2.	Generally does not deviate or get sidetracked from the task at hand.
( )	( )	( )	3.	Does not get frustrated when stymied, but figures out another approach to achieve the same objective.
( )	( )	( )	4.	Has a past record of completing assigned tasks far above average.
( )	( )	( )	5.	Is a team player, not overly concerned with who gets the credit so long as the objective is obtained.

( )	( )	( )	6.	When an occasional job is very difficult, tries persistently to complete it.
( )	( )	( )	7.	Relates well to superiors, avoiding any temptation to make derisive comments in their absence.
( )	( )	( )	8.	Is respected by those who report to him/her with few legitimate gripes heard from any subordinates.
( )	( )	( )	9.	From all outward appearances, enjoys a stable homelife.
( )	( )	( )	10.	Seemingly receives adequate emotional support from family members in the pursuit of his/her career.

Totals:

( ) ( ) ( )

Total each of these three columns. For each column, a total of 42 and above is Excellent; 36 through 41 Good; under 36 Unsatisfactory. Are you satisfied with your rating? If not, this scale might help you gain some insight as to needed changes in order to become a more successful executive.

Of course there are always some factors beyond our control, as any executive or business manager will readily admit. Sometimes these culminate in unique stress facing today's work force known as the syndrome of "job burnout."

Job burnout is a concept applied to situations where people experience physical ills, become emotionally upset, or are troubled with family problems, all arising from too much job pressure. Job burnout affects everyone—employers as well as employees. When individuals regularly dread getting up each morning and going off to work because of job frustration or unhappiness, job burnout may be the cause. In these situations people have experienced high levels of job stress, but have been unable to cope satisfactorily with it. As discouragement rises, a breaking point is reached after which the individual withdraws, failing to interact or cooperate other than minimally with fellow-workers. Job burnout, then, is a pattern of behavior which is a reaction to job stress.

Other symptoms include exhaustion, both emotional and physical, and doing only enough to get by at work. Many executives may experience a loss of idealism, failing to perceive their positions or progress as exciting and challenging. Sometimes burnout victims are plagued with physical symptoms, including sleep disturbances, high blood pressure, headaches, and all types of gastrointestinal problems, such as ulcers. Even back and neck pains become legitimate physical complaints for those suffering from the psychophysiological stresses resulting from burnout.

Factors believed important in contributing to job burnout are a lack of control over one's work pace, schedule, or environment. This lack of control can apply to the pieceworker involved with a continual monotonous task, but it also affects the high-level executive who must answer to a board of directors, defend payment of a lower dividend in spite of rising sales due to surging operating costs, while fending off union demands for a larger slice of the shrinking pie. With so many factors beyond his or her control, the executive feels helpless. Lethargy may take over where once there was exuberance! Executive hooky may be indulged in, with the executive taking every opportunity to be absent from the office.

An even greater concern for the executive undergoing job burnout is the discovery that burnout is contagious! Cary Cherniss studied job burnout, publishing his findings in a 1980 *U.S. News and World Report* article, "Job Burnout: Growing Worry for Workers, Bosses." Cherniss found that such workers were more likely to become cynical, negative, and pessimistic. Since these workers were formerly leaders in their sections or units, it was not surprising to discover that soon the entire work force assigned to that division became victims of job burnout.

Job burnout follows no set schedule, affects new as well as old workers, and is found everywhere in the work force, including the executive suite and on the assembly line. Though it is impossible to establish a set timetable for burnout, Dr. Bruce A. Baldwin suggests five stages as burnout progresses:

Stage I:	Intimate Involvement
Stage II:	Exhaustion/Questioning
Stage III:	Balancing Act
Stage IV:	Withdrawal/Disappointment
Stage V:	Terminal Cynicism

The first stage involves the newcomer over-identifying with the job and putting undue emphasis on anticipated fulfillment. Most people enter new adventures expecting far more than is possible to gain from the experience. This is reminiscent of the old axiom that no job is ever as good as anticipated before it begins nor as bad as it seemed after it is over. During this period when initial interest peaks, the new worker tends to be too idealistic, looking at the perspective job through rose-colored glasses. This period is appropriately thought of as the "honeymoon phase" of job adjustment.

Exhaustion and questioning begin when a person becomes overextended and too involved with the job. The toll is both physical and emotional, with the worker feeling fatigued in spite of adequate rest; he or she experiences one or more of the psychosomatic burnout symptoms referred to earlier. Questions relating to self-confidence arise, such as, "Am I capable of hanging on to this position?" or "Am I equal to the demands and pressures of the job?" This may be followed by wistfully eyeing other jobs and wishing another profession or some other field had been chosen. At this point it is imperative to remember that while we readily recognize both the strengths *and* limitations in our own chosen job, we can only glimpse the strengths or attractions in fields untried, creating an unfair comparison at the outset.

Critical decisions are made in the "Balancing Act" stage, sometimes consciously, at other times subconsciously. These choices determine whether burnout will be arrested or proceed to a more critical stage. Deciding to balance the importance placed on the job and career development with family and other leisure interests represents an important crossroad. Individuals must first determine what constitutes success, i.e., wealth, position, reputation, or power, because from this basic premise comes self-esteem or a sense of self-worth. Also involved is the emphasis placed on family life. Part of a definition of success must include quality parenting and healthy family relationships. Furthermore, physical health cannot be ignored or any success achieved will be tainted or short-lived.

Withdrawal and disappointment begin when an adequate balance hasn't been established or maintained between commitment to the job, family, health, or outside pursuits. This may be signified by withdrawing from others, both at home and at work, getting less accomplished though spending even more time on the job, moderate-to-severe depression, or boredom as workdays assume a sameness with one day becoming as uninteresting and boring as the next.

In the final stage of "Terminal Cynicism," the person suffering from burnout turns inward, protecting rather than managing the self. Cynicism takes over, accompanied by resentment, with a shift of priorities from work to nonwork interests, ending with a sense of failure and worthlessness. Is there a solution to job burnout once it has reached this final stage? Of course, but it may require intensive short-term counseling, which should be considered by anyone suffering with these feelings.

Generally speaking, burnout is least likely to occur where the individual has the freedom to exercise personal control over his or her effectiveness within the workplace. For employers, there is a need to structure jobs so that the personnel can play a more meaningful role in determining how the work is approached. This means less rigidity in the work place and though there are some exceptions, where allowances cannot be made without jeopardizing the firm or its product, these remain just that—exceptions. In most instances individual job initiative can and should be encouraged. It will make for a happier work force, and perhaps even a more efficient team, as individuals exert more control over the manner in which their jobs are accomplished.

Of course, job burnout is not the only source of stress in the executive suite. It is now widely accepted, following conclusions from several studies, that executives are more likely candidates for heart attacks, high blood pressure, cancer, and suicide than is the general population. The question most germane to those in corporation executive suites a-round the country is "Why?" Stress is believed to be a chief cause contributing to, if not causing, most disease in men and women. Once we believed specific stress-related diseases occurred primarily in males; but recent studies show that for executives, females in policy-making positions are as likely as males to experience such diseases. Still the question is left unanswered, "Just why is stress more likely to exact its high toll from the business executive than from others?"

R.I.P.

"R.I.P." conjures up an abbreviation of "Rest in Peace," often chiseled on small tombstones, especially in frontier days. In today's world, however, business executives need to think of "R.I.P." as the main cause of both physical and psychological stresses in the executive suite, where "R.I.P." stands for:

1. Responsibility
2. Intensity
3. Pressure

1. *Responsibility:* The sign displayed on former President Truman's desk is appropriate for the business executive: "The buck stops here!" Executives are responsible for de-cisions affecting the lives of those working under them, their company's survival, and their own economic livelihood. Such responsibility is awesome, and at times the weight of this demand must seem unbearable. Outside activities which provide a release and pleasure are essential for executives who feel harried by the demands of the responsibility in their positions.

There is no room in the executive suite for the work-aholic's prideful thought, "I've done it all myself." Cooperation, interdependency, and teamwork are the hallmarks of the modern successful executive or businessman. Though the "self-made man" alleviates the Almighty of an awesome responsibility, as the wag suggested, it is an invalid concept for the modern business or corporate executive who knows better.

2. *Intensity:* Those who take pride in claiming, "I spend eighty hours a week on the job," are deluding themselves regarding their productivity. Not many are capable of sustaining the necessary intensity for success beyond forty-five hours each week. Large corporations recognize intensity as an important trait in executives, but also recognize that a periodic change in environment is necessary if the person's productivity is to continue. Many companies own or lease vacation quarters where top-level management can relax and regather personal resources prior to returning to the executive suite. Though the intensity of total commitment is generally important to the success of any endeavor, *no one* can maintain high-level, intense involvement without some relief and relaxation.

3. *Pressure:* The pressure executives work under directly contributes to their levels of stress. Stress is inherent in all areas of life. In fact, a certain level of stress is absolutely necessary for people to achieve their desired goals. What is often not recognized is the need to control the *level* of pressure-producing stress—especially for the business executive. Pressure can be controlled if alternatives are available to, and used by, the executive. Better-adjusted executives develop aides who can accept primary responsibility for certain areas under their direction. Executives can further control pressure by maintaining open lines of communication with peers and subordinates, enabling them to call for

help when needed. Successful business executives recognize that a legitimate call for help is never a sign of weakness, but rather one of strength.

Attention to responsibility, intensity, and pressure — direct contributors to negative stress in the executive suite — should enable executives to keep their individual levels of stress manageable.

Coping with Executive Stress

Excessive stress becomes internalized as distress, with consequences affecting the body. Ulcers are common reactions for those executives unable to cope adequately with stress. The body's chemistry is thrown out of balance, with the stomach's acidity rate rising to dangerous levels. Perforations in the stomach's lining are the end result of untreated ulcers.

Executives need to pursue a sound physical exercise program several times a week. In addition, wise corporate leaders develop a relationship with someone away from work where total candor can be shared about job-related anxieties and concerns with no fear of creating further problems at work. To assist in this regard, some businesses provide major executives with regular counseling sessions by outside psychologists. These professionals are not responsible to the companies, but rather help the executive sort through his or her priorities, resolving any seeds of potentially paralyzing anxiety in an atmosphere of total confidence.

Married business executives who have continued to nurture adequate communication with their mates through the years have additional confidants to serve as "sounding boards." Gone are the days when executives took pride in "never bringing work home." Actually, concerns from the job have *always* been carried into the home, probably more often covertly than overtly, as business executives are aware.

Anxieties and work-related concerns produce stress which is not only brought home but is carried into all other settings as well. The only adequate way to defuse work-related anxiety is to ventilate it by making use of a combination of physical exercise for the body and mental conditioning for the mind. An understanding mate or close friend may be one of the executive's best mental conditioners against being overcome by too much stress.

Stress Can Help You Be Your Best!

While you cannot avoid stress, it can be used to help you be your best as long as you take care of both body and mind.

Naturally all of us have different capacities when it comes to coping with stress. Some executives cope best with occasional high levels of stress arising from a particularly excessive demand in their jobs, while others work methodically on a more even keel, though not necessarily getting less done. Executives of equal ability have been known to thrive on high stress levels, yet some react strongly even to minor problems.

Stress activators which prepared primitive man to face dangerous animals in order to protect his family and home continue with us today. The problem is that in our prehistoric form, once the danger abated, so did the stress which prepared the body for "fight or flight." In today's business world, stress may be activated several times in an eight-hour period yet never be thoroughly resolved. Consequently some managers are more apt to make poor decisions late in the day, primarily because they have exhausted themselves due to elevated stress levels. Essentially, they stayed on guard too long for the dragons that never came.

Executives and managers at all levels recognize that most job stress today is psychological, with anxiety and worry driving up blood pressure, causing the heart to beat more rapidly. Tension increases at a rate that soon becomes overwhelming. Where stress is created by a condition which is beyond control, the corporate leader should reduce as far as possible all other stress in his or her life. This can be done in a variety of ways, including exercise and learning self-help techniques which can be easily acquired in a brief seminar.*

Among the variety of ways to reduce stress is to make a list of all events causing you stress, ridding yourself of those you can. If a chief problem exists in constant clashes with a close associate, put as much distance as possible between the two of you. Staying available for the "good of the other" seldom proves beneficial to either person. Cutting losses before the strain becomes too great is the best way to reduce or eliminate such stress which undoubtedly causes distress.

Increasing your daily exercise will culminate in the body building and storing up energy throughout the working day. When a job involves physical labor, an overload of stress can be worked out via exertion of energy. This is not so for a desk job. Taking regular walking breaks each morning and afternoon in place of that coffee break will dispense with much of the excess energy that adds to body tension and hence increases stress. Participating in tennis, jogging, handball, or consistently "working out" at a gym or health spa, especially where swimming is available (which is one of the best forms of exercise and body toning) will go far toward dispelling excessive stress build-up on the job. (Review "Exercise" section in chapter two.)

---

*"How to Turn Stress into Success" is the title of a seminar which has proven helpful to many corporate employers and employees across the country. For more information, write Dr. William D. Brown, Suite 217, 1025 Connecticut Avenue, N.W., Washington, D.C. 20036 or call 202-833-8792.

As a leader you will want to "be kind to others, for everyone is fighting a hard battle," as Alexander Pope reminded us, but do not overlook using some of your energy to apply this principle to yourself. You fight a hard battle to keep up with the demands of your job, and occasionally you need a complete break from office routine. Don't be afraid to take an afternoon or day off to walk the beach, visit an attraction you have long wanted to see, or just relax in bed reading something of interest (non-job related) or watching television episodes. Diversity is an important way to renew both the energy and drive necessary for good management.

Evaluate yourself: do you tend toward perfectionism in the demands you place on yourself and your subordinates? Perfectionists are never happy because their goals are unrealistic; neither they nor their subordinates will ever achieve or live up to their unrealistic levels of expectations. This leads to constant frustration for employees, but worse yet, leaves the perfectionistic manager in a continual state of frustration. Remember, everything is *not* worth doing well! *Some things simply aren't worth doing,* and others only need marginal attention. Reserve your energy investment for those tasks that need to be done well. Less stress will be generated for everyone.

If you are one of the legions of top managers who beneath an exterior of "having it all together" actually feel unworthy of your position, you are probably suffering from low self-esteem. At an American Medical Association conference Dr. Walter Bortz of the Stanford Medical School placed greatest importance on one's attitudes, as these affect the individual's well-being. He was speaking specifically about aging, a concern of most managers who realize how rapidly the years seem to be advancing. Dr. Bortz stated, "Negative attitudes toward aging can seriously damage the human organism. The human body should last up to 120 years but it wears out much earlier because people are even more terrified of growing old than they are of dying."

We are using the wrong comparison of self-worth when we compare ourselves with the youthful set, without wrinkles, varicose veins, paunchy stomachs, and graying hair. Mid- to upper-management should have long since moved beyond worship of the physical as the proving ground for self-worth. Self-esteem should be found in the quality of life enjoyed, the way personal accomplishments are rated, and how much realism is embodied in your future goals. This is a healthier backdrop against which to measure your self-esteem and a far better gauge of your true self-worth.

Stress must be faced at every level. Executives and managers do well to remain aware of, and stay in sensitive contact with, the world around them. Remember, you have a tremendous effect on those people reporting to you, who are often left hanging on your every word. If you are in the habit of cheerfully greeting employees each morning but become preoccupied one day, slighting a worker, the latter may fret over it the entire day and actually produce less work.

Another pitfall for executives is shutting themselves off from other people, even those in their firms. As they are promoted and move higher up the corporate ladder into more responsible positions, more means become available for insulating themselves. Such insulation arises when just a few lower-echelon personnel report directly to the one at the top.

Amazingly, much stress is brought on by an executive's success, which causes a special type of stress. Once people achieve major goals, they may no longer feel the need to work as hard as they did earlier. The constant tension experienced on the way up the ladder of success may no longer be present. Once success has been achieved, there may be a letdown. If new goals are not established, complacency can result in lethargy or an "I don't care" attitude. This is where the pursuit of the goal is more gratifying than its actual attainment. Unfortunately this is usually recognized only by the twenty-twenty vision of hindsight.

Another stressor may be felt by the newly successful person who feels he or she should adopt a different life style. This is seen best when one is promoted over others. The question then arises, "How should I act now towards them?" The relationship seems to change for all parties when a peer or equal becomes a superior. Of course, those left behind may claim to note more change than has actually occurred. Various acts may be interpreted as "putting on airs." What isn't noted is the insecurity felt by the newly successful one, which occurs simply because he or she *has* become so successful.

In addition, the successful ones may feel different—even guilty—because of their good fortune. These feelings raise anxiety far beyond stress levels which are adequately handled. Sometimes the easiest recourse is to withdraw from others. The assumption that successful people tend to change is correct: success *does* change people—at least somewhat. However, we must go beyond describing such change, looking for its reasons instead. Interpreting signs of "superior" behavior can be deceiving. What may be interpreted as superiority may actually mask feelings of inferiority, such as, "I wonder why I have been so successful?" or "I wonder if I can live up to the success I have achieved?" Successful people are very much in need of emotional support. More compassion and understanding is needed in corporations, not only from the top down, but from the bottom up.

Lack of proper verbal communication is felt to be a primary cause of job failure, from board chairmen not getting their intended messages across to stockholders to mid-management erring in assuming foremen understand explicitly the job requirements. This may leave those employees at the lowest echelons operating in a vacuum of understanding just what *is* expected of them! Where does this inability to communicate begin? Probably in the home, where all stress starts, as was noted earlier.

Home is where the art of communication is refined. This is true whether you live with family or friends. If you live with family members, your communication with these most significant others in your life serves as an effective gauge measuring how well you communicate verbally on the job. If you cannot communicate well with those who share your life most intimately, you will not be well-equipped to interact verbally with people outside the home. Those who are able to share their deepest feelings with their mates, other family members, or even best friends, develop the skills most necessary to communicate effectively on the job. In the business world this can mean the difference between success and failure. It does no good to have the best product, plan, or idea, unless you can effectively communicate it to others.

While directions and ideas must be correctly related, for a work environment to be productive and successful, feelings of openness and regard for other individuals must also be accurately communicated. Stress Inventory XI will be a great help in this regard. Six key phrases are given which should be practiced at least twice a day for three weeks, both at home and on the job. After twenty-one days, they will become so ingrained that they will be a part of your subconscious thought patterns. In time you will notice an appreciable difference in the way you relate to others and their open acceptance of you. In addition, your cultivated interest in them will shift from an experiment to that of genuine interest!

Stress Inventory XI
Most Important Words

Memorize all six phrases. Next, practice using each of the six at least twice a day for the next three weeks, both at home and at work.

Six most important words:
"I'm sorry, I made a mistake."

Five most important words:
"You did a good job."

Four most important words:
"What is your opinion?"

Three most important words:
"If you please."

Two most important words:
"Thank you."

One most important word:
"We."

An employer once said, "I don't *get* ulcers, I *give* them." That might be fine as braggadocio small talk at cocktail gatherings. However, in reality, an employer who deals with employees from this point of view is bound to have problems, such as an organization where the absenteeism rate is high, workers who are resentful toward "the boss," and generally a less productive firm because one fundamental principle has been forgotten: *"People don't really care how much you know until they first know how much you care."*

Simultaneously recognizing and alleviating too much stress among employees will help keep management stress at a minimum. Watch for the following symptoms in the workplace as indicative of excessive work stress:

- Low morale
- Poor staff communication
- High job absenteeism
- "Turf wars" among the staff
- Fear of making decisions
- Excessive worry over taking risks
- Low productivity

Such signs need to be dealt with immediately, for the quicker they are eliminated, the healthier the companies will be.

For employers, the big temptation to avoid is establishing neurotic relationships with their jobs. This occurs when an executive fails to separate his or her personal identity from the corporate position, so that work becomes all-pervasive. These are the work-prone people we refer to as "workaholics."

Christopher J. Hegarty, in a *U.S. News and World Report* article, maintained "(Workaholics) often can't distinguish between valid work and validating the fact that (they) are executives."[1] Many men who no longer need to be finan-

131

cially involved in the business on a daily basis have, over the years, developed an insatiable "need" to be needed on the job. Hence, they feel worthless if cut off from work, though in reality they now go to the job for the sake of work rather than any returns from their efforts.

This type of behavior is not limited to business owners in the private sector. Many corporate executives are caught up in a maze of paperwork—memos piled on their desks, computer printout sheets stacked on the floor—giving no thought to improving their work methods but, when falling behind, simply resolve to work harder and longer. Hence, workaholism becomes part of the problem rather than the solution. Companies are sometimes penalized by people who work too hard and spend too many hours at their jobs as they tend to become flat, lacking inspiration and imagination in tackling the tasks at hand. When creativity becomes stifled because of too much work, or one's perception of too much work, the actual return to the firm on its investment in the individual is low.

Surprisingly enough, compulsive workers are not necessarily unhappy people, though their devotion to work can present real problems for their spouses and children. The problem arises because these workaholics are happiest when putting in long hours with the first love of their lives—their jobs. In order to maintain peace at home, it is important for the workaholic to be honest: workaholism is not a disease, but rather a condition caused by desperately wanting to overachieve.

There is nothing wrong with being achievement-oriented, working many long, hard hours if proper priorities are maintained. These include time for outside interests, meeting the needs of a growing family, and devoting enough time to one's spouse.

If you are a workaholic, there are some guidelines which will help you maintain the delicate balance in your life. First, involve the family in what you do. Dr. Marilyn Machlowitz in *Workaholics* advises introducing family members to co-workers. Also, take the children to your work place to let them see where you spend so much of your time while away from home. Further, definitely keep communication open with your spouse about what is going on at work. The worst mistake is to shut off family members from your work world so that they feel isolated and alienated. Take care that you don't view yourself as indispensable on the job, for logically this isn't true. No one is. Ironically, those who feel indispensable at work seldom see themselves as indispensable to their families, yet in reality they are more likely to be irreplaceable at home, where their role as spouses or parents are unique.

If you cling to the notion that you are indispensable at work, remember the message contained in the following poem:

The Indispensable Man

Sometimes when you're feeling important,
Sometimes when your ego is in bloom,
Sometimes when you begin to think you're the most
* qualified in the room,*
Sometimes when you think your going would leave
* an unfillable hole,*
Just follow these simple instructions and see how
* they humble your soul.*
Take a bucket and fill it with water,
Stick your hand in it up to the wrist,
Pull it out, and the hole which remains
Is the measure of how you'll be missed.
You can splash all you want as you enter,
You can stir up the water galore.

133

But stop and you'll see in a moment, it looks
quite as calm as before.
Now the moral of this quaint example is
"Do the best that you can!"
Be proud of yourself, but remember—
There's no indispensable man!

—*Anonymous*

Finally, what is needed is a critical look at the life style you've developed. Ask yourself the question, "Do I work in order to live or live in order to work?" Workaholics seldom realize they have shifted from an industrious role to one of enslavement to their work. When this realization does occur, it frequently comes too late. Children have grown, spouses departed. However, family members can help workaholics lead balanced lives if they will rechannel some of their energies. Hopefully, talking with loved ones will help them reevaluate those things most important in life. Thinking through life's priorities should result in a healthier perspective for workaholics.

Because of the unique stress faced by upper management, loneliness is an important stressor. Many researchers feel that a strong network of social and family ties is most important in coping adequately with stress. When these ties are broken, such as in divorce, studies have shown that there is an increase in the incidence of heart disease, strokes, and even infectious diseases such as tuberculosis.[2]

Mobility places unusual strain on both executives and their family members. When transferring executives, many large corporations use relocation firms to smooth the transitions. Also, some firms are beginning to offer the family members counseling in conjunction with a job move, especially when teenagers are involved, as they frequently find it most difficult to pull up roots and relocate.

Family solidarity becomes crucial to the executive who has been dismissed from his position. Because mid-level to top management people have so much of themselves invested in their work, when dismissal — the corporate equivalent of divorce — occurs, it is especially important that they be able to find solace within their families.

There are many reasons why an executive may be fired which do not reflect on his or her ability to do a job well. For example, in corporations when a new chief executive officer is appointed, changes may be made in the management team to fit a new and different work style or philosophy.

Hopefully in the future more firms will join those enlightened corporations which now recognize that firing executives is an occupational hazard of big business and carries no stigma either for the firm or individual. The next step is to make readily available procedures for helping these executives to start over.

Ultimately, like all other groups and segments of the population, there is no more escape from stress for employers than for anyone else. However, putting into practice the foregoing ideas will help any executive be better prepared to cope with the inevitable stress of the corporate world. Dealing successfully with stress can even become a game, turning problems into opportunities, which can bring great pleasure to the executive who rightfully prides himself as a problem-solver.

·8·

Unique to Employees

At first glance, it would seem relatively easy to categorize people as either employers or employees. Employers are people who hire employees to work for them. So far so good, but what about those who are both employers *and* employees? Nearly everyone works for someone else, including the chairman of the board who answers to his directors or stockholders, the clergyman who is responsible to his parishioners and possibly an ecclesiastic superior, the physician who must satisfy his patients, and the businessman who works to please his customers.

Essentially we could conclude that there are no absolute categories of employers or employees. Nearly all jobs are a combination of the two. Further, there is much crossover in many offices between employer and employee roles. Workers find themselves filling the role of employers with several people answering to them, while viewed as employees by those who supervise their work. Socially many employers and employees associate freely with one another both on and off the job. This involves planning special work events, participating in outside company-sponsored competition such as bowling, softball, or physical fitness programs, and visiting in each other's homes. These are healthy contacts provided care is taken to avoid becoming overly dependent emotionally on another in the work force. When this happens, there are negative effects which irreversibly change employer/employee relationships.

When Jane first came to work, she was responsible for handling correspondence for three executives. One was abrasive while another was aloof. The third, Tom, was attentive, considerate, and understanding. An almost instant rapport was established between the two. Gradually each looked forward to coming to work more than going home at the end of the day. They confided in each other about their respective mates, children, and home life. This mutual trust and respect blossomed into a full-blown relationship with all attendant emotional and sexual interplays neither had planned. Both being mature people, each promised the other that regardless of this new development in their relationship, their professional lives would not change. They believed they could keep their personal relationship separate from their nine-to-five professional lives. It wasn't long before it became painfully obvious that such expectations were unrealistic. They jeopardized their jobs to such an extent that shortly after leaving their respective mates, each was fired because of poor job performance. Further, what had begun as a mature relationship between an employer and employee ended adrift on a sea of accusations, recriminations, and charges that ended their personal relationship.

Developing personal relationships on the job generally causes more problems than the people involved envision. Those who would reply, "But we couldn't help ourselves," should be reminded that no behavior just happens: *all behavior has a cause.* If the cause which attracts one to another employed in the same office is so strong as to be irresistible, it would be better in most instances if one of the two sought employment elsewhere before the relationship blooms.

Daily emotional turmoil in the work place brings distress to everyone involved. Each person, employers and employees alike, must assume responsibility for contributing to a positive work atmosphere. Consider the following poem as an excellent measure at the end of each day:

> *Someone started the whole day wrong —*
> *Was it you?*
> *Someone robbed the day of its song —*
> *Was it you?*
> *Early this morning someone frowned;*
> *Someone sulked until others scowled;*
> *And soon harsh words were passed around —*
> *Was it you?*
> *Someone started the day aright —*
> *Was it you?*
> *Someone made it happy and bright —*
> *Was it you?*
> *Early this morning, we are told,*
> *Someone smiled and all through the day —*
> *The smile encouraged young and old —*
> *Was it you?*

> *—Author Unknown*

Although employees can suffer from too much stress, they may also suffer from *too little* stress. Insomnia, loss of appetite, irritability, and excessive crying are characteristics of boredom and frustration from work underload. As Dr. Tobias Brocher of the Menninger Foundation explains, "There's been too much generalizing about stress. Stress is not necessarily bad. We all need some stress, and it is possible to suffer the same distress from underload as overload." This is typically experienced by young professionals, recent graduates, who are straining at the starting point to immerse themselves in their work, only to be held back by a conservative employer.

Another one likely to be vulnerable to distress from underload is the worker involved in repetitious, monotonous tasks, such as an assembly line worker. The late stress authority Dr. Hans Selye felt that people are basically motivated to achieve. Underload is usually a condition forced on workers early in the career process, with some people readily accommodating themselves to its low-level demands. Still, these same workers can, and do, suffer from stress, experiencing much boredom.

Though job boredom is easily predicted in a job where the routine seldom varies, few of us stop to realize that routine is also a large part of jobs we consider exciting—the airline pilot, the highly respected professional, or even the social director on a cruise ship. When we daydream, the Walter Mitty emerges in each of us as we become the pilot who safely lands the troubled plane, the physician who has just expertly removed the brain tumor, or the cruise ship hostess dancing away the final evening of the excursion on the ship's ballroom floor. We don't identify with the complaint of many pilots that flying a plane is a job crammed with hours of tedious boredom, occasionally punctuated by moments of stark terror! Before performing a successful operation, the physician has devoted hours to preparing the patient for the ordeal, and postoperative care has a certain quality of sameness seen in all patients. Even the cruise ship hostess spends countless office hours on specific details responsible for an event's success.

Job success usually requires devoting energy to those tedious tasks that make the more interesting hours possible. What is needed is to handle job boredom constructively whenever it arises. In recent years employment specialists have recognized that many people need to change vocational fields several times during their working careers. It is possible to become so bored with a job that a worker suffers from burnout, a condition where interest is lost in work and there is little enthusiasm for anything in life, as discussed in chapter seven.

Changing employment can be beneficial in such instances, and, if you find that you are bored most of the time in your work, perhaps a job change should be considered. However, another alternative is to develop methods of offsetting inevitable job boredom. Playing mental games, imagining yourself off on a trip, reliving happy past experiences, or savoring future anticipated activities are safe ways to ward off job boredom.

Unfortunately, too many people choose to alleviate job boredom by using mood-altering chemicals. An example would be the assembly line worker who, when the conveyor belt stops, uses coffee, cigarettes, alcohol, or pills to counter boredom. A healthier response would be to become active in pleasurable diversions after work, creating a "natural high." These might involve pursuits in music, sports, games, or solitary pastimes such as fishing, walking in the woods, or meditating. The importance of finding a fulfilling avocation should not be overlooked by those suffering from stress underload.

Too much stress, however, whether due to over- or underload work levels may cause the individual's arteries to constrict and blood pressure to elevate. Meanwhile, glands are also secreting increased amounts of the nerve-stimulating chemical epinephrine into the system. Repeated reactions to stress such as these can cause individual breakdowns in the body's functions, incapacitating the individual or even resulting in premature death.

Stress responses vary widely. Some body systems develop an immunity to the usual stress-related physical symptoms, emerging from high stress situations unscathed. (For instance, statistically, people whose spouses have died are twice as likely to die within a year as other people their age, supporting the assumption that emotional distress causes or contributes to body changes resulting in early death.) However, as has been suggested, the intensity of stress may be less important than the way in which it is handled.

Perhaps the key factor in coping with stress affecting employees hinges on a strong network of social and family ties. A break in these ties appears to increase incidences of heart disease, strokes, and even certain infectious diseases. Actually little is known about the causes of stress or its effects, leaving the worker only with the assurance that (1) stress is real; (2) it is universal; (3) it won't (and shouldn't) go away; (4) we must learn to live and cope with it, recognizing that (5) one's avocation may be even more important than one's vocation in sustaining a sense of fulfillment, especially when a strong network of social and family ties is maintained.

Of course, for any specific person it may be that the present working situation is not one for which he or she is best suited. Regardless of the benefits, if the pressure is too great, it is unwise to remain on the job, even if the counterpoint is, "But I could never make this much money anywhere else." Anyone who works solely for money is underpaid, regardless of how much he or she earns.

If a manager is unreasonable, the employee must look for ways to reduce job pressure, thus making it possible to remain on the job. Such an approach might begin with an understanding of why the boss is difficult. While this won't change the behavior, it can change the employee's attitude and hence his or her response toward the behavior. Though categorizing people is difficult, as noted in chapter three, Drs. Friedman and Rosenman in their work concluded that there are three basic types of individuals: Type A, Type B, and a mixture of the two. Approximately 50 percent of the American male population is Type A, 40 percent Type B, and the remaining 10 percent a combination of the two.

Employees need to be reminded that many bosses are Type A personalities; they tend to be intense, ambitious, and aggressive. Their competitiveness goes beyond the work situation; most are unable even to approach games without an intense urge to win. Type A bosses feel constant pressure to expand their areas of influence, to improve the quantity of their work (often via the employee), and to make the office increasingly more productive. Impatient, they constantly fight deadlines and may speak with machine-gun rapidity, ending sentences in a rush. They interrupt others, feel they have no time to get sick or take vacations, and are preoccupied with work. Rushing through life, they never enjoy the moment at hand. These are primary candidates for coronary diseases, which they frequently view as an unjust reward in view of their "virtue" of hard work.

Surviving in an office under a Type A boss isn't easy, but it can be done. Accepting that he or she is a victim of that particular personality type may be helpful. Next, it would be beneficial to work at escaping the work setting. Some suggestions for easing the stress in those situations are:

1. not taking boss's tirades personally;
2. using relaxation imagery; and
3. assuming responsibility for your own attitude.

Attitude is all-important. Mentally you possess the ability to avoid constant exposure to job pressure though on the job eight hours a day. Recall the astute observation of William

James, the professor of psychology, physiology and anatomy at Harvard University around the turn of the century who noted:

> The greatest discovery of my generation is that we can alter our lives by altering our attitude of mind.

Of course, a certain level of job stress is important for the employee if any progress is to occur, for without it there would be no enthusiasm and motivation. Determining your own optimal stress level is all-important. Dr. Rosalind Forbes, founder of the Forbes Associates Stress Consultants of New York City and author of *Corporate Stress* maintains, "The optimal stress level is the one which got you where you are today in terms of your life and your career. When you have that optimal stress level, besides being enthusiastic and motivated, stress gives you an energy; it helps you to think more clearly. The mental abilities are heightened because of that slight spurt of adrenaline in the body, and that's where the energy comes from, too." Workers who are most likely to succeed are those who have the ability to make stress work *for* them, handling it productively while channeling it into their work.

A surprise is usually encountered by those guessing which jobs cause the highest levels of stress, who list corporate executives, doctors, or police officers among the most stressed. However, according to the National Institute for Occupational Safety and Health, laborers top the list, with secretaries in second place. Other occupations among the most stressful include waiters and waitresses, farm owners, and office managers. These people are most likely to respond to a psychological-physiological emergency system referred to earlier as the "fight or flight" response—an automatic way of responding to trouble, suspected or real, which involves both the mind and the body. The response begins within one to five minutes, bringing the body to a high level of energy. If this level isn't brought down within twenty-four hours, it begins a cumulative effect on the muscles of the body, especially the heart muscles. This tends to wear down the muscles and blood system, eventually affecting the digestive system, leading to indigestion and possibly ulcers. This suggests that workers experience greater job stress than executives. Why?

One reason is that executives can delegate stressful duties to subordinates while enjoying fringe benefits that offset the stress of their work. Additionally, executives have control over their jobs while workers under them exert little if any job control. Fortunately, exceptionally high levels of job stress can be reduced by employees when they work at means of controlling blood pressure and heart rate through use of stress-reducing techniques.

How much is too much in terms of job stress? Dr. Michael S. Haro devised the Tension Quotient Test, presented below as Stress Inventory XII, as one means of answering this question.

Stress Inventory XII
Tension Quotient Test*

To test your tension quotient, respond to the statements below. Assign them a value from 1 to 5 based on how they most clearly relate to your behavior (1-Never; 2-Seldom; 3-Occasionally; 4-Frequently; 5-Always). When you are finished, add up your points and find where you fall on the risk scale.

Type A Personality

1. I am tense.

2. I am highly competitive.

3. I am plagued by deadlines.

4. I am subjected to many stressful events (homelife, work, financial, etc.)

Autonomy

1. I enjoy being unattached to people or things.

2. I resent people who try to regulate my conduct.

3. I could live in a very lonely place.

4. I would enjoy being my own boss, working alone.

5. I consider myself to be independent and free.

To score:

  4-8: Little to no risk.
  9-12: Low to moderate risk.
 13-16: Moderate to high risk.
 17-20: Potential problem
      or crisis.

To score:

  5-10: Little to no risk.
 11-15: Low to moderate risk.
 16-20: Moderate to high risk.
 21-25: Potential problem
      or crisis.

Anxiety

1. I feel anxious and tense.
2. I am afraid of such things as being alone, experiencing new things, being in crowds or closed places.
3. I am restless, uneasy and/or unable to relax.
4. I wake up too early and/or am unable to stay asleep.
5. I have weak feelings and/or shakiness or dizzy spells.

Aggression

1. I do my best not to let people get the best of me.
2. I feel that certain people need to be put in "their places."
3. I let it be known when I am angry.
4. I get angry at myself and other people.
5. I experience instant anger if things don't go as I had planned.
6. I let people know when they do something I do not like.
7. I tend to criticize others under any circumstances.

To score:

5-10:	Little to no risk
11-15:	Low to moderate risk
16-20:	Moderate to high risk
21-25:	Potential problem or crisis.

To score:

7-14:	Little to no risk
15-21:	Low to moderate risk
22-28:	Moderate to high risk
29-35:	Potential problem or crisis.

*From Haro, Michael S., "T.Q. and What It Can Mean to You." Houston, TX, 1981.

Note that because a person scores in the moderate to high risk category does *not* mean that stress itself is the problem. It may be that an individual lacks the ability to cope adequately. When all one's energies are expended coping with stress, there is little energy left when an additional crisis hits. Everyone needs a plan to determine those things that really count, avoiding worrying about life's irrelevant events or happenings.

In his book *Kicking Your Stress Habits,* Dr. Donald A. Tubesing, a Minnesota psychologist, suggests a repertoire of coping techniques which employees should find helpful. First, *organize your time.* Figure out when in the day you are most productive, confining your essential and important tasks to that time. Pace yourself making certain that diversions are built into your day, for as the commercial proclaims, "You deserve a break today," and a break every day from the sameness of work-related tasks, regardless of how interesting.

Next, *follow what Dr. Tubesing designates as "clean living."* Don't overindulge in eating and drinking; get adequate rest to offset fatigue which reduces one's ability to cope with stress, and reverse the typical American meal pattern by eating a large breakfast, a moderate lunch, and a simple supper.

Let your body be your barometer. Obey the messages it conveys. When the body sends a message that it is exhausted—a pain begins in the neck and head, the back aches, or the stomach gets upset from having been "tied in knots"—turn aside to another pursuit, at least temporarily.

Do those things which are most important, the things that really count. Putting emphasis on what is most important can be a good way to convert stress into eustress, rather than distress.

Don't be afraid to make a choice between fight or flight. Either approach is necessary at times, though often failing to move at all appeals to most of us. The resulting problem is that stress internalized is far more harmful than we expect. A passive-aggressive pattern emerges which does little to soothe either the individual or close work associates. Later, these buried resentments surface, often at the most inopportune time, causing friction far in excess of what would have occurred if the problem had been addressed initially.

Most of us need to get outside of ourselves more often. Sometimes, when overly stressed, people turn inward, focusing too much on their own problems. Our own perspective of personal problems is too limited, causing us occasionally to overlook obvious solutions. Finding a trusted friend, seeking out a chaplain if one is available, or turning to professional help is far preferable to keeping everything bottled-up within.

Finally, as Dr. Tubesing suggests, *don't make the mistake of living for the day when you will be free of problems,* or when life is going to change dramatically. Chances are your future will be similar to your past. What we should change is our ability to appreciate and savor what is most important in the present, for as long as we live we will experience stress. The secret to job contentment, as is the case in other areas of life, is learning to cope more satisfactorily with the inevitable stress found in every line of work. As Adela Rogers St. Johns put it when describing her own struggles with the stresses of life, "I learned to be happy *in spite of* things, not *because* of things."

Complaints are often heard that American workers are taking less and less pride in their work. The president of the advertising agency, Batten, Barton, Durstine, and Osborn, noted in a recent issue of *Marketing News:* "We are in the Age of Me, with its hunger for personal success, money, and personalization." He went on to characterize the times as "an age of self-interest rather than self-sacrifice: 'I want to be me'; 'I'll do it my way'; or 'I love me and why not?'" The problem with this approach is obvious. If one's interest is turned totally inward, the worker will not take pride in the job he can do, but rather in what the job does for him. Today it isn't so much an absence of pride but rather a shift from pride in the way the job is done to priding one's self on how the work (in terms of rewards) benefits the worker. Multiplied many times over, such thinking affects not only the individual but industry as well, ultimately destroying our collective pride in "Made in America."

Job burnout, as discussed in the previous chapter, is not limited to employers or employees, is no respecter of age, length of service, or profession. It can be found in nearly all fields. Dr. Eli Glogow of the University of Southern California's School of Public Administration noted, "It's hitting education, business, all kinds of public and private sectors. It's a terrific waste of manpower and it's increasing." Unfortunately, as with executives or managers, what causes burnout for one worker will not affect another. Yet prime candidates for burnout are teachers, medical personnel, secretaries, and working wives, to name but a few.

Often the public school system is a citadel of stress. Overworked and underpaid, teachers face a number of difficult situations. The demands of working in a hostile environment where there is little public or administrative support cause personal pressure. In addition to deteriorating disciplinary and academic standards, budget cuts have reduced many of the materials and services teachers formerly relied on. Also, many have to work two jobs to support their families.

Under such conditions mental attitudes and professional performances begin to deteriorate. As the pressures mount, an escape from classroom teaching is sought. It is common for teachers to seek almost any administrative position within the system to avoid continuing in the classroom. Further, many valuable teachers are now seeking other professions. Dramatic action is needed to reverse these situations and trends before public education, the chief cornerstone of our republic, erodes beyond repair.

Medical personnel are another group hit hard with job fatigue and burnout. Some researchers feel burnout in this field is more crucial than in any other, due to threatened patient care. Because of the interdependency between the emotions and physical health, less time spent with the patient by hospital staff can retard healing or assisting the patient in getting well. Of course in extreme cases judgment is impaired and decision-making ability reduced, leading to errors that could cause life-threatening situations. Dr. Pamela Patrick, author of *Health Care Worker Burnout: What Is It, What to Do About It,* a former registered nurse who was a victim of burnout herself, believes it is the product of long-term chronic stress brought on by work-related problems rather than by personal difficulties. Further, she believes those in the "helping professions," including teaching, social work, and law, are especially vulnerable because of their deep involvement with the problems of others. Medical personnel, including physicians and support staff, frequently find it difficult to change readily from dealing with patients to interacting with others, such as their family members. Experiencing almost cultural shock phenomena when shifting between the two, many need a break, an emotional decompression chamber, to help with the transition from a hospital setting to the home. Activities which might prove beneficial in this regard include walking, running, or other forms of exercise, reading, meditating, or any one of another of the stress reducing techniques. (For more specific recommendations, see Davis, *et. al., The Relaxation and Stress Reduction Workbook* listed in the bibliography.) Job burnout for medical personnel can be reversed, but much effort is required to keep it from becoming an all-pervasive factor.

Secretaries are another group prone to job burnout. Unfortunately, it is believed to be the powerlessness of secretaries on the job which causes them to rank so high in at least one category indicative of stress, that is, coronary disease.

In the Framingham study, Dr. Suzanne Haynes, an epidemiologist with the National Heart, Lung, and Blood Institute, found that although working women as a whole do not have a higher rate of heart disease than housewives, women employed in clerical and sales occupations have coronary rates twice that of other women. Since more than one-third of all women work at clerical jobs, this is a large percentage of the entire work force. Secretaries who actually develop heart disease are often those with bosses who don't support them in office politics, women who had little opportunity of upward mobility and are now trapped in dead-end jobs, and those who have difficulty expressing anger. A large portion of their inhibitions may have been directly attributed to the lack of control they felt they had over their jobs, and indeed their lives. This problem can be accentuated when their bosses feel stymied, so they express their need for job control by exerting power over their secretaries. Subsequently, not only are these bosses in danger of suffering heart disease from too much stress, but they are also dispensing a high level of stress which all too often frequently causes the same for their secretaries!

Automation is one of those mixed blessings experienced in the modern office. While it removes much of the previous boredom and tedium from office chores, similarly it leads to robot-like, desensitizing job skills to operate the machines that increase clerical frustration. This is especially true when these same clerical workers feel manipulated by the demands of the new machines which have invaded modern offices in the last ten years.

One of the problems is that many of the clerical workers are over-qualified for their present jobs. Having started in jobs which seemed challenging, they soon mastered work requirements only to find there was nowhere else to go, as the jobs were dead-ends. Lacking further vocational challenges, these employees grow increasingly irritated and frustrated, which causes them additional problems when the stress levels become intolerable.

Many secretaries would do well to reexamine their jobs to see if they fulfill their professional needs. If not, other vocations should be explored. No one should feel trapped in any endeavor simply because "This is all I know!" Change remains inevitable in all areas of life; the working world is no exception.

Ms. Paula I. Robbins in her book *Successful Midlife Career Change* observes that many workers are deciding to have more than one career in a lifetime. She advises a four-step process to be followed in making a job switch. First, take time to assess your skills, both strengths and weaknesses, writing out a complete work history. Second, analyze all previous jobs held, the paying as well as the nonpaying. Rate yourself on the things you did best as well as those where you didn't fare so well. Third, translate the conclusions given above into an occupational goal. What do you want to do for the rest of your working days? This should then be matched with existing jobs in the working world to see what employment prospects there are for doing what you would most like to do. Fourth, draw up a job resume, stating your job objective in a single sentence with back-up facts. You might also contact a nearby community college, inquiring of adult-continuing education programs designed to assist individuals in career changes, especially in midlife.

Another group suffering from special stress is wives who work outside the home. Attempting to manage a family while simultaneously juggling a job causes unique problems apparently not experienced by husbands, who for the most part work outside but avoid chief responsibility for running the home. One study found women managers four times more likely to seek psychological help than were their male counterparts. Constantly feeling they must prove themselves on the job, these women experience rejection from a lack of acceptance in the business world.

Men, of course, are more likely than women to have spouses at home full-time or be married to mates who assume most home responsibilities. This appreciably lightens the load for the working male, while the working female finds she must not only compete adequately in the business world, but also maintain a functioning household for other family members. Add to this the factor of unequal pay for equal work performed, and it is easy to recognize the special stresses faced by working wives.

Just how important is spouse support to one's career? Most mates would probably agree it is impossible to calculate the importance of their mates' support in their work, which is as important for wives as for husbands. Those who receive such encouragement are those far more likely to succeed in the business world, for it is difficult enough to be successful with a business endeavor even when all else goes right.

When a person is threatened by his or her spouse's work and therefore is reluctant to be supportive, the chances of that spouse succeeding are considerably lessened. The non-supportive mate may feel hostile for personal reasons. However, left unresolved, this hostility could grow, affecting other areas of a relationship, eventually destroying it. Anger causes people to respond illogically, even when they realize their actions are harmful.

Of course the ultimate in job rejection is for the employee to be let go, terminated, or fired. Never a pleasant experience, not only is it a blow to the ego, but it causes high levels of stress and anxiety. "How will this affect my future employment?" is a reasonable concern. "Will others view me as a failure?" is another fear. Some firms are providing separation counselors with whom released employees can talk through their feelings concerning the deflating experience of having been fired.

One of the most valuable support roles at the outset is that of listener, which is important for loved ones of the dismissed employee to remember. A key term here is "transition." It is important to view current circumstances as transitional rather than terminal. Panic is not productive! Employees do well to recall that several studies have shown that employees dismissed by one firm tend to find improved positions at another. When one is fired, humiliation is normal and should be expressed. This is a time for reaching out to friends and colleagues for support.

Looking for a job while feeling anxious and insecure is most difficult. Take stock of yourself honestly. Admit blame for your mistakes, but don't accept *all* the blame. Some conditions are beyond the individual's control and should be viewed as such.

Employment even in temporary work can be an excellent bridge leading back to permanent employment in your desired field. Sometimes employees feel there is something degrading about temporary work, but it is far easier to move from one job to another than to make that difficult transition from the world of the unemployed to the employed.

Because unemployment carries a stigma, most companies tend to look more favorably on hiring you if you are currently working, even if the job is not one you would prefer or carries less status than one you had earlier.

Most importantly, there is no such person as one "born to fail." If people were born to fail, those born in the worst circumstances would be destined to experience failure throughout life, but history attests to many individuals who have overcome tremendous handicaps to achieve success. Conversely, those born with all advantages the "right" family can afford are not guaranteed success.

Failure is not a respecter of persons or class. Indeed, failure is encountered by virtually everyone. Clichés are sometimes overworked, such as "When the going gets tough the tough get going!" Though this thought has served to motivate many, it cannot be applied universally. Perhaps sometimes we are not tough enough, or it may just be *too* tough to be tough. In any event, no matter how many times we do not succeed in our pursuits in life, we are *not* failures. Indeed, you cannot be a failure, for *failure is an event — never a person!*

Many people, even though employed, feel a sense of failure or internal unrest. Though they may try to analyze the reasons why, they may not recognize the value of a clear conscience. For example, when answering an inquiring conscience with a glib "Sure I cheat. Doesn't everyone?" it is only temporary balm for having violated their own code of ethics. Knowing the difference between right and wrong but failing to act on this distinction is certainly a cause of stress in the long run. To determine the stress your conscience may be causing, carefully examine each item in Stress Inventory XIII.

Stress Inventory XIII
An Ethical Inventory

Answer each of the following items either True or False. Then check your rating with the key offered below.

_____   1.   I have never cheated on a test or examination of any kind.

_____   2.   I have not lied to anyone about anything in the last month.

_____   3.   I have never passed off another's work as my own.

_____   4.   I would never knowingly accept overpayment in change from a clerk.

_____   5.   I have never attempted to cheat the telephone company.

_____   6.   I have never been paid for work I didn't do.

_____   7.   I have never taken any item from a hotel/motel not intended to be kept by guests.

_____   8.   I have never overstated a claim to an insurance firm.

_____   9.   I have never failed to tell the whole truth when filling out my income tax forms.

_____   10.   I have never knowingly misrepresented any item in order to make a sale.

Count the number of statements you marked True. Use the scale as follows:

9 to	10	—Highly developed conscience
7 to	8	—Above-average conscience
5 to	6	—Average conscience
3 to	4	—Below-average conscience
1 to	2	—Conscience needs help!

Even though we are able to "convince" ourselves at the conscious level that we aren't doing anything anyone else wouldn't do if given the chance, this form of rationalization doesn't "wash" at the subconscious thought levels. Consequently, there is little escape for one who knowingly cheats. The conscience exacts a high price for wrong-doing, even if no one else ever knows about it.

To be a good employee or employer requires an ethical code that does not take unfair advantage of others. Reducing stress and ridding ourselves of potential distress requires discarding the temptation to be less than honest with others or ourselves. Because employees and employers face many similar stress-producing situations, you are encouraged to read again chapters seven and eight for a thorough understanding of reducing job stress.

Part Three

Turning Distress into Eustress

·9·

Distress Gives Way

Mary was passed over for promotion in her office. Better educated than the male who was selected, she also had more experience, had been told she would get the job, and had assumed responsibility for many of the duties describing the higher position, receiving two letters of commendation from her superiors during the last six months for her high-level performance. She was demoralized on learning that the board had selected one of its own members to fill what she had thought would surely become her position in the firm. Hurt, resentment, and depression took their toll during the first twenty-four hours after she had received the shocking news. These then merged into feelings of anger and resentment as she wondered how she could strike back at her superiors, the firm, its executive board, and the person chosen to fill "her" slot.

At this time, her stress level reached a turning point: it could become distress or eustress, depending on her reactions and subsequent actions. Deciding it wasn't worth a fight, she continued with the firm for another six months, but slowly lost interest in her work, failed to arrive in the office on time more often than not, assuming an "I don't care" attitude which soon forced her to leave the company "by mutual consent," the announcement read. Mary's stress turned into distress, ending not only with the loss of her job but also leading to increased smoking and drinking away from the office. Within two years Mary was dead, death attributed to an overdose of abused drugs coupled with excessive alcohol detected in her blood stream, according to the coroner's report.

If stress is permitted to get out of hand, the resulting distress can lead to alcoholism, drug abuse, or even suicide. The primary question to consider is whether Mary could have avoided her bitter disappointment over being passed over for promotion? Probably not. She would have been expected to experience some distress, as keen disappointment. However, there were other avenues Mary could have chosen. Once her initial disappointment and anger had been worked through and subsided, she could have taken positive action. For example, she could have directly confronted her superiors, eventually taking her case to the chief executive in her firm if necessary. Of course she may not have received that promotion or a similar one within the firm, but taking action, rather than remaining passive-aggressive, would have helped turn her distress into eustress.

Not much is known of Mary's life style, but she could have handled stress better had she been following a regular regime away from the office including setting aside time each day for something relaxing, an enjoyable pursuit in which she could become immersed even if only for short periods. Next, she should have been adhering to an exercise program at least three to four times weekly. Not only would this have helped keep her physical body in shape, it would have assisted her in sleeping better and, in general, feeling good about herself. Trying to limit the number of other stressful situations in her life would have enabled her to channel more of her stress into eustress, for there are fixed limits to the amount of stress that we have either the energy or will to handle at any one time.

Above all, keeping change to a minimum in life during especially stressful situations is important. In Mary's case, she only compounded her level of distress when she took less interest in her work, pulled back from her former role as a responsible worker, with a resulting negative change in attitude. Everyone has a breaking-point, as was proven in most recent years with our POWs in the indescribable conditions of North Vietnamese prisons. Admiral Jeremiah A. Denton, now U.S. Senator from Alabama and author of *When Hell Was in Session,* was the senior officer in his prison compound. In spite of all previous training, Denton noted, the enemy was able to "break" the U.S. officers repeatedly by using torturous methods. The fact is *anyone* can be broken if the stress level is accelerated enough.

Refusing to play the "if only..." game is another way to turn distress into eustress. "If only..." permits us to loll in the luxury of what could have been if only we had invested in IBM in the late fifties, bought a house years ago when prices were much lower or had seized some other lost opportunity.

Substituting "and yet..." for "if only..." raises the chances of succeeding with any task, for emphasis is placed on what can be done *now* as opposed to what might have been. In his profound book, *Reality Therapy,* Dr. William Glasser emphasizes starting from where you are with what you have. Rather than returning to the past, wasting time figuring out how you got where you are, Glasser's therapeutic approach is to confront you there, help you view your options realistically, and then give support in choosing a course in light of these options. Regardless of what has occurred in your life, distress can be turned around, as you pick up and continue from where you are, rather than stagnating over some error or mistake from the past. This is not to deny the multiplicity of problems facing individuals or society, but it does recognize that we are not without hope.

Let's turn now to examine some of those specific problems which have a high potential for distress that we might become more aware of ways to channel stress directly into eustress.

One can hardly think of stressful feelings without conjuring up the concept of love. Growing into or falling in love can be stressful, but nowhere nearly as stressful as growing out, or falling out, of love. The rejection factor in the latter is more than some can bear. The lovelorn stumble along blindly until time helps heal the wound, or circumstances present other options.

The pain of being rejected is not related to age, but to the person's ability to deal with difficult situations. For example, parents sometimes make the mistake of assuming that teenage love is not to be taken seriously, when in fact it is at this age people can be most vulnerable to painful feelings of love and least equipped to cope effectively with them.

Most people, regardless of their ages, don't know how to deal with unrequited love or love which has ended. Escaping a failing love relationship with one's self-concept intact isn't easy, for failure here is usually seen as a personal failure.

The support of friends and family who will be good listeners can help the stressed individual shift feelings of sadness or hostility to indifference. Taking positive action—exercise, new activities, etc.—rather than dwelling on "what might have been" is another useful technique.

Anxiety is another cause of distress which can be avoided as we learn to identify it and turn it into a creative force.

Mild anxiety is normal for all of us, whereas intense anxiety hampers people in their work, play, study, and relationships.

Many psychologists and psychiatrists agree that women are particularly susceptible to anxiety. Dr. Helen De Rosis in her book, *Women and Anxiety,* feels that because women have undergone upheavals in their role developments in the recent past, many have become dependent on mind-altering drugs to alleviate or reduce anxiety. As a psychiatrist, Dr. De Rosis believes this same anxiety could be channeled into a positive life force. Anxiety produces "energy units" in the body, creating a nervous, "motor-running," sensation. According to Dr. De Rosis:

> (Anxiety is a) feeling of dread...a constellation of
> physical symptoms, of uncomfortable, troubled feelings
> and thoughts that may be relatively mild or reach the
> point of utter panic. (This) reaction to frustration and
> to unresolved anger seems to burn a hole into your
> very being. It is a response to unbearable stress. It is a
> beacon light signaling the existence of unconscious
> emotional conflict.

Anxiety is produced by differing and opposing goals which are incompatible when one attempts to fulfill both roles at once. Examples include the working mother who desperately wants to succeed in her job outside the home yet would like to fulfill the super-mom myth, or the loving father who is torn between the need to spend hours on the job and his desire to be at home with his children.

De Rosis's twenty-step anxiety-management program centers on picking a time to work when you won't be disturbed, recording your feelings in a notebook. Select an issue causing you anxiety, determining how this issue makes you suffer. Be specific with your examples. Write down ways you have tried to deal with it. Do you want to risk trying to make a change? If uncertain, make a list of possible losses and gains resulting from such change. Choose a possible solution, putting it into action. Later evaluate this new action in terms of losses and gains, selecting another solution if the first was ineffective, then repeating the evaluation processs.

Divorced people frequently experience high levels of anxiety and stress, especially when they feel "single" status was forced upon them against their wills. This can cause anger and hostility if not resolved. Recognizing divorce as fraught with danger, some clergymen are assisting couples in ending their unworkable marriages with divorce "rites." Standing before a clergyman with family and friends looking on, the couple recites special pledges, leaving the altar with the minister's blessing. While some claim that a divorce ceremony contradicts the church's emphasis on love and marriage, others feel it is an idea whose time has come.

The Reverend Doctor Robert Elliott, professor of theology at Southern Methodist University, claims churches add to the pains of divorce by frowning on couples who separate. "Divorce is the only major life trauma for which the church has no ritual, no rite of passage to help a person symbolically traverse the dangerous passage from one stage of life to the next, to let go of the ties to the old," he says. Somewhat akin to a funeral, divorce rites afford a catharsis, a ceremonial ending, helping a couple close the door on a failed marriage with the assistance of loved ones and friends.

Elliott concluded a service he performed by stating, "You are set free to face new futures as separate persons. Carry no burden of guilt or recrimination for what is past. Accept grief as it may come, but release the past into the past and receive the future of God's gift of new possibility." This approach can help a couple avoid distress, especially where children are present. Once divorced, however, parents face a new and special kind of stress—single-parent stress.

Though stress in family settings is hardly unique, single-parenting is more difficult than co-parenting, since the single parent has to assume total responsibility for tasks once shared in a two-parent home. This is difficult even with everyday tasks, such as getting children off to school or working an outside job while running the home.

In addition to the difficulties of the daily routine, there are often special situations for the single parent:

• Martha finds it most difficult vacationing alone with her seven-year-old daughter. Only recently divorced, she cringes each time her child remembers "experiences" to share with daddy upon her return home, refusing to accept that daddy is no longer there. When daddy does come to visit, he brings expensive gifts, which Martha worries will make her daughter materialistic.

• Bob occasionally becomes distressed that he hasn't enough time for his nine-year-old daughter. Due to the demands of his job, he is away from home for long periods, fearful that the sitter is making more of an impression on his daughter than is he. While he does some dating, he is not interested in remarriage at this time though he sometimes wonders if his daughter wouldn't be better off if she had a good feminine role model at home to follow.

• In financial straits since her divorce, Jean and her two teenagers moved in with her mother. Three generations under the same roof cause special problems, with Jean having to mediate between her young sons and her mother. There is little privacy now, with constant reminders that she is living in someone else's house. "This has by far been my most difficult adjustment," writes the forty-four-year-old mother.

Though rearing children alone generates a lot of stress, most unattached parents would choose being single over living in an intact home where tension and hostility prevail. Still, facing life without the moral support of another adult can cause intense stress. Consequently, some find it helpful to pool their efforts and resources. Those with very young children trade sitting time among themselves. For example, babysitting hours may be recorded so that the sitter has credits banked for future use. This is especially attractive when a large group of single parents live close by.

Self-help groups such as Parents Without Partners (PWP) have been lifesavers for many singles. Parents in these groups find understanding and empathy. By being involved with others like themselves, self-confidence grows and loneliness lessens. Single parents should never be ashamed to seek help when needed. Only then can they adequately cope with the stress of rearing their children by themselves, turning potential distress into eustress.

Couples who remain married to the same partner year after year face problems of their own. Since any couple faces occasional distress with each other, how do they keep it from ruining their relationship? Are there secrets these couples have discovered that others have missed? "Life is never easy for anyone" is a cardinal rule we all understand, yet most of us conjure up images of the lives of others, believing that surely they have it easier, better, or are happier. Though intact marriages aren't necessarily signs that all is well for either partner, some couples have found ways to reduce marital stress. One of those "secrets" is to emphasize things which brought them together initially. Another way to reduce stress and help a good marriage is via the popular Marriage Encounter programs which have spread across the country in the last decade.

Marriage Encounter is a highly structured weekend which attempts to shut out the modern world while teaching a married couple how to communicate better to each other their thoughts and feelings. Often while undergoing this process they are able to discover a relationship which has been buried under layer after layer of job, family, and other everyday pressures. The result is a deeper appreciation and understanding for each other which either was never present or had never surfaced.

Originally created in Spain by Father Calvo, S. J., in 1967 the program was introduced in the United States. Today it involves ten faiths in all states and forty-six foreign countries. It is estimated that over one million husbands and wives have attended Marriage Encounter programs. Some of the more widely known groups sponsoring or affiliated with Marriage Encounter programs are the Catholic, Episcopal, Jewish, and ecumenical organizations formed solely for arranging Encounters.

"Presenting" couples who previously experienced a weekend give twelve to fifteen talks to audiences of twenty to thirty-five couples following a step-by-step talk outline. Couples separate after each talk for a quiet time, writing down their feelings about the topic and questions just covered. Not a problem-solving weekend, it is designed as an introspective experience with emphasis on building from the present.

The program is mainly for good marriages, attempting to improve them. Much emphasis is placed on couples communicating openly with one another. Many feel this process has helped them relate better to their children. Those who have gone on an Encounter weekend believe it is something a couple has to experience to appreciate, with almost universal praise coming from couples who have participated in these programs.

While Marriage Encounter aids communication and fosters togetherness, there is no intention that couples should spend time only with their spouses or feel guilty when pursuing healthy activities outside the marriage. No marriage is able to fulfill adequately *all* one's needs. We are more inquisitive and demand a greater challenge from life than can be provided exclusively by another person. Friends with whom we can bowl, play cards, attend club or lodge meetings, or other forms of recreation not of any real interest to our mates, are essential.

Such freedom within a marriage helps to strengthen it and might be one answer to the doomsayers distressed about the future of the American family as an institution. Certainly the American family is experiencing one of its gravest attacks in our young history as a nation. Will most people live together without benefit of marriage bonds in the future? Is marriage—and hence the nuclear family—a dying institution? Can we expect divorce to continue increasing at such a rapid rate that serial monogamy—where one marries several mates in a lifetime, though one at a time—replaces traditional monogamy, i.e., one man married to one woman for life? Also, what about parental roles? Isn't there already evidence of a role upheaval for some fathers and mothers, with house-husbands staying home while their wives go to work outside?

Let's examine the whole picture both for causes of distress or eustress regarding the future of the American family.

The increased flow of wives into the work world is expected to continue, even if inflationary demands for two incomes per family are lessened. Many women have found they can juggle working outside the home while keeping the house running and will be reluctant to give up the economic advantages or intellectual stimulation of outside employment following the early morning exodus of husbands and children.

Adult females are worthy of the same consideration as adult males. As noted earlier, the historical mistake of assuming the woman was better off in the home, keeping her constant vigil was not only illogical but irrational. Many homes suffered from wives and mothers who resented being isolated from the world of ideas and trapped within confines of their four-bedroom, two-bath enclosure on a 50' x 100' parcel of ground. When females have the freedom of choice as to how to spend their lives, the whole family benefits, from the youngest to the oldest. When parents are satisfied with themselves, they are more fit for the demands of parenting. *Individual fulfillment is not a conflicting goal with parenting, but rather a prerequisite to parenting adequately.* As more mothers work outside the home, the number of "latch-key" children will increase, that is, those children left on their own after school. This situation can cause distress for both the parents and the children, but is the distress inevitable? Surely through our ingenuity we can devise safe, secure, and constructive alternatives for the children during the two-or three-hour period before an adult returns home.

A greater problem for the future of the family is the increasing number of children being reared in single-parent homes. If the divorce rate continues at or near its current level, this means that almost *half* of all children born today will live with only one parent during at least a portion of their early years! Homes tend to procreate themselves, meaning that family relationships in one generation seemingly beget similar family patterns in the next. Therefore, it is of prime importance that children be exposed to family settings, or intact homes, where individuals are respected and accepted for their unique talents, as opposed to how well a standard family role or mold is filled regardless of personal qualifications. In this way, children will be encouraged to appreciate family life in the future, with accompanying freedom for family members to be themselves.

Shrinking households as an American trend is expected to continue. In 1930 there was an average of 4.1 persons per household in the United States, but today there are only 2.8 persons per household with a bottoming out yet to come, according to demographers. Further, there is a record number of people living alone, according to the latest Census Bureau figures. In 1970 only 3.7 percent of American households had but one person present. Today 22 percent of the households are comprised of one person, consisting of the young, divorced, or the old.

Any changes in these trends is dependent on future economic conditions. For example, unless families in America are willing to double up, with young married couples moving in with one set of parents, unavailability of affordable housing is expected to result in fewer early marriages, smaller families, and possibly a lower divorce rate, as marriage will increasingly be entered into by the more mature.

Another positive expectation from these changes in the American family is a lower juvenile delinquency rate. With a lower birth rate and children born to more mature families, presumably parents will have ordered their priorities differently, placing more emphasis than they did in the past on closer contact with their offspring. This should mean fewer youngsters left on their own, with better parental supervision leading to better discipline while at the same time producing a moral or ethical code which will help youth distinguish between right and wrong. Dr. Mark W. Cannon, administrative assistant to the chief justice of the

United States, observed this need in an address before the Southwestern Judicial Conference when he said:

> Though alcoholism, poverty, and perceived social
> injustice all contribute to crime, there is a deeper force
> that is causing a breakdown of our society. These
> merely tip the raft of social order, while a deep current
> is moving the entire raft at a startling speed. That deep
> current is our failure to transmit positive values,
> norms, and attachments from one generation to
> another.

Alexander Solzhenitsyn went even further when he spoke at Harvard University, recognizing the tremendous effect of spirituality and religious commitment upon society. He stated:

> How did the West decline?...I am referring to the
> calamity of an autonomous, irreligious, humanistic
> consciousness...It will demand from us a spiritual blaze.

In the recent past there has been a diminishing emphasis on ethics and values taught in our public schools. The Thomas Jefferson Research Center, a nonprofit institution studying America's social problems, reports that in 1775 religion and morals accounted for more than 90 percent of the content of school text-books. By 1926, the figure was only 6 percent; today it is practically nonexistent! Concurrent with this shift away from moral/ethical emphasis in the classroom, many homes pay little attention to religion, seldom even mentioning the subject. Albert Rhodes and Albert Reiss in their article, "The 'Religious Factor' and Delinquent Behavior," ran elaborate statistical analyses before concluding that boys with no religious preference committed *twice* as many crimes per thousand as those who had a religious preference.

Drs. Engeman and Benson writing in *Amoral America,* observed:

> Contemporary western society suffers from inadequate
> training in individual ethics. Personal honesty and
> integrity, appreciation of the interests of others,
> non-violence, and abiding by the law are examples of
> values insufficiently taught at the present time...Our
> thesis is that there is a severe and almost paralyzing
> ethical problem in this country...We believe that we
> can demonstrate that unlawful behavior is in part the
> result of the absence of instruction in individual ethics.

But where are ethics to be instilled? In the home or in the school? Why not both? Testifying before a House subcommittee in 1979, the Honorable Charles E. Bennett stated:

> The home and the church can no longer be solely
> relied upon. Today they are least available where most
> needed. These institutions today are no longer
> equipped to handle the job without help from our
> schools. Those children who are most in need of
> instruction are getting it least.

Yet, many argue that teaching an ethical code requires the intrusion of religion into the classroom, which they feel has been outlawed. However, note carefully the Supreme Court's rule banning *classroom prayer* in its 1962 ruling:

> It might be said that one's education is not complete
> without a study of comparative religion or of the
> history of religion and its relationship to the
> advancement of civilization. It certainly may be that
> the Bible is worthy of study for its literary and historic
> qualities. Nothing we have said here indicates that
> study of the Bible or religion, when presented

objectively...may not be effected consistently with the
First Amendment. (Engel vs. Vitale)

Though prayer in the classroom was ruled unconstitu-
tional, *religion as a classroom subject was left untouched.*
Unfortunately, there has been very little attempt at public
teaching of religion, possibly due to confusion by educators
and parents as to what is permissible. Yet, failure to do so
penalizes our youth tremendously. They graduate from our
public education system with a thorough knowledge in the
arts and sciences, yet with no understanding of religion and
its moral effect on individuals and societies. Can our individual and collective stress be lessened until we address
this issue? I think not.

Still there is good reason to be optimistic about the
morality of our young people. In a 1980 poll of *Who's Who
Among American High School Students* (Twelfth Annual
Survey of High Achievers, 1980), 24,000 respondents re-
vealed the following hopeful picture:

- Eight out of ten belong to an active religion with 71
  percent attending services regularly.
- Nearly half don't drink and 88 percent have yet to
  smoke their first cigarette.
- The vast majority (94 percent) of these teens have
  never used drugs, including marijuana.
- Eighty percent do not think pot should be legalized and
  90 percent wouldn't use it if it were.
- Regarding sexual intercourse, 76 percent of these teens
  have not had sexual experiences.
- Over 86 percent of those surveyed favor a traditional
  marriage as opposed to relationship experimentation
  which has been in vogue in certain youth circles in
  the past.

- Some 52 percent watch fewer than ten hours of television a week, counter to existing studies of their lower achieving peers.

These are encouraging statistics, suggesting a resurgence of positive leadership roles among the very group that will help lead the way in the future development of our nation.

Because of the need to love and be loved, families will continue to be taken seriously as one of the primary sources available to fulfill this need. Mary Jo Bane, co-author with fellow Harvard professor George Masnick of *The Nation's Families: 1960-1990,* stated: "People still need one another." Because the world exposes us to brutality, hurt, and discouragement, the family becomes even more important as a sanctuary where we can withdraw from the din and clamor of the outside world. Carl Sandburg expressed it this way: "Home is the place where when you have to go there, they have to take you in."

Change continues exacting its price on everything. The family is no exception. What we need to do is determine what we want from our families, neither idealizing nor neglecting the past in the process. For one thing, disciplined people are happier than the undisciplined masses; this rule applies to the family as well as to society itself. Also, adolescents need to become contributing family members once again, finding themselves and a sense of direction in the process. Many adults feared this purposefulness was permanently destroyed by our bent toward permissiveness which created havoc in the lives of so many youth in the most recent generation. They were never taught to distinguish between freedom and license, and now many are enslaved by the very practices that at first they believed signified freedom.

All in all, the resurgence of positive values and directions leads to optimism about the family's future in America and goes far in alleviating the dismal distress felt by so many in the last decade.

Another issue which is a growing cause of distress is a preoccupation with physical health. Though most of the public worries about cancer, the number one killer in America is not cancer but heart disease. Chapter two offers many ways to combat heart-damaging stress, arising both from physiological and psychological causes. Another way to manage stress is to relax via a process of biofeedback techniques which can significantly reduce high blood pressure and other factors linked to heart attacks.

Biofeedback techniques include training in relaxation, i.e., breathing exercises, deep muscle relaxation, and mental relaxation in the form of meditation. These devices create physical changes thus enabling the individual to reduce the negative effects of stress. Since no drugs are used, biofeedback has no harmful physical side effects, and once mastered, the learned responses can be turned on and off at will to deal with stressful situations such as standing in line, sitting in traffic jams, or a host of other pressure situations beyond the individual's control.

One of biofeedback's greatest assets is that patients themselves are being called upon to share the responsibility for their own health care. Biofeedback training has also been instrumental in helping patients lower their cholesterol levels, smoke fewer cigarettes, and suffer less anxiety, all considered contributory, if not primary, causes leading to high incidence of heart disease.

Retirement is yet another source of distress for many people. Planning for retirement often becomes a mental stumbling block, as such planning is associated with death. With the will to live ingrained in most younger adults, retirement seems a preparatory stage leading to the loss of life. However, without planning and preparation too many retirees become rudderless ships, adrift from one day to the next with no sense of purpose or direction.

Conversely, for many people a chief problem with retirement has been the unrealistic expectation that retirement years would be glorious and golden—and that somehow this would happen automatically and effortlessly. Yet, as we have seen, nothing happens without cause. Planning effectively for retirement is just as important as the preparation one makes prior to entering a career, for retirement is but another phase of one's career. With proper planning and forethought, men and women *can* look forward to retirement with confidence and even excitement. Then, as these expectations are established mentally, retirement can indeed be golden, underscoring once again Dr. Karl Menninger's assertion, "Attitude is *always* more important than fact."

Like the question entertained by children—"What do you want to be when you grow up?"—adults obviously need to give prior thought to *"What do I want to be when I retire?"* and then set a plan in motion that will result in a personally satisfying, new life style. An effective retirement plan must consider not only future financial needs, but also the broader physical, social, emotional, and spiritual ones. Feeding the whole person is as important in retirement as in any other stage of life. Establishing goals for retirement in mid-life is not premature, for prior planning eases the transition from working to retirement years.

When planning for retirement, consider your physical health. Are there special problems restricting the climate where you should live? Do you have physical problems which will need attention from medical specialists who are concentrated in a specific geographical area? What types of exercise will you take up in retirement? How will these differ from past physical activities?

Social friendships need to be closely examined when approaching retirement. Many friendships are job-related, so once a person is retired, these are difficult to maintain. Plans must be made to cultivate new friendships in a variety of new social and special-interest groups. Loneliness is the curse of retirement, especially for those who move to new areas and are unable or unwilling to take the necessary initiative to acquire new friends.

When thinking of retirement, we might consider: how well adjusted emotionally have we been throughout our working years? This is a good indicator of how contented and satisfied we will be in retirement. Those involved in constructive pursuits, hobbies, athletics, community activities, church affairs, and the like, are fortunate to have found many sources to feed their emotional needs.

Also, maintaining a disciplined life in retirement is very important. Time spent wisely is a good investment in sound mental health. Sitting back, letting one day blend imperceptibly with another, is unhealthy. At that point a person is existing, not living. The better adjusted retirees are those who continue to feed *all* their needs; retirement becomes the chance to pursue a rich variety of activities.

How one adjusts to retirement depends not so much on leaving work but on how well the individual adjusts to change. Retirement represents a major life style change. Those who don't get unduly upset over change stand the best chances of adjusting satisfactorily to retirement. Recognizing one's limitations is always important. Some do not accept change easily, which is a direct cause of high stress. These men and women may curse retirement while those who adjust more easily to change would most likely welcome it.

Just as important is the life style of the individual approaching retirement. One who is already active in diverse pursuits may not find much change in retirement. Those who say, "I don't know how I ever had time to go to work," fall in this category. So does the woman who stated, "I never knew how much I was missing in life until I retired. Now I choose what I want to do, and it is far more rewarding than my thirty years of full-time work."

Remaining active is apparently the key to enjoying fulfillment and longevity in retirement. When one who has been busy in a job retires and does nothing, his or her life style can be compared to a freight train roaring down the tracks coming to an emergency stop. Fortunately, there are countless opportunities awaiting the retired. For example, there are organizations dependent on volunteer labor, many offering individuals a chance to work directly with others. Also, the Small Business Administration has need of retiree services in consulting with self-employed persons. This is a program where retired businessmen give their time in helping advise active businessmen.

Retirement housing alternatives are another important consideration. Rather than giving up a single-family residence to move in with relatives or a boarding home, retiring couples or singles need to explore creative approaches. Some retirees have profited in several ways by taking in boarders who help meet their financial needs of continued upkeep on a large house, provide some companionship, conversation, and enable them to avoid stark loneliness.

Even for those with limited income in retirement, housing futures are not necessarily bleak. One option worth exploring is having adult children help retired parents maintain separate housing via some monthly financial contribution, or if this is not possible, searching out suitable "housemates" through church groups or other friends. Sharing expenses with another may allow both to live independently.

When both husbands and wives are present in retirement as hoped for, such couples should consider themselves fortunate. Are there trips they wanted to take in the past, places to go, or relatives they had hoped to visit, all foregone because of the pressures of work? Such deferred gratification is no longer necessary in retirement. If adequate funds are available, retired couples can share in some of life's richest experiences, enjoying activities only dreamed about in the past.

Single retirees have to develop more ingenuity in planning for retirement, but with the increasing number of single retirees, more people are available with whom similar interests can be shared. Overcoming the stress of meeting new people or facing strange situations will certainly be offset by the stimulation and pleasure one finds. Having a positive attitude and taking action are the keys.

To say that death can cause distress is obvious. Some even argue they can see distress giving way to eustress in all instances except death. Just how does one cope with the death of a loved one? How is it possible to redirect this distress? Often dramatic change occurs following the death of close family members. Chaos within the family may result at such times.

One problem in coping with the death of a loved one is that its aftermath frequently leaves survivors feeling totally helpless. This may be the "can do" generation, where man can fly to the moon, to some extent control the weather, invent intricate machines to do much of the tedious work, and can train surgeons to perform delicate operations which exceeded the imagination only a few years ago. Yet, faced with eliminating death, man is utterly helpless, approaching the future with considerable uncertainty.

This helplessness can lead to frustration which is sometimes converted into aggression, with family members venting their frustrations against one another. The aggression is real, though individuals are left dissatisfied, since this is hardly a productive outlet for the distress they feel.

Rather than avoiding each other following the death of a principal family member such as a parent, the surviving family members should be encouraged to come together and support each other, especially during the period immediately following death. If signs of dissension arise, family members should address the situation immediately. Ignoring the problem will only make matters worse. When left to fester, imagined or real wrongs will assume even greater magnitude. The point is that this kind of change is never easy. Family members should not try to continue living as if nothing momentous has occurred. Emotional healing may be needed during their delayed reaction to death. Such a healing may be helped by a sensitive family member or friend who is understanding, compassionate, and tactful.

One of the most devastating losses of all is the death of a child. Bereaved parents need understanding and support during their grief. Compassionate Friends, founded in 1972, is a group of parents who gather to help ease one another's pain. At these meetings, some of their despair and distress is blunted as they share their grief with others who have had similar experiences, seeking both to give and receive comfort. Talking about being unable to get up each morning and face a new day, wanting to scream inappropriately and even to throw things in the process of relieving their pain are not unusual topics at a gathering of Compassionate Friends.

Bereaved parents report that while they can talk about their child's death to close friends and relatives who sympathize but who cannot really understand, turning to a group where members have suffered similar experiences offers far greater comfort. The only structured part of any meeting is the introductions, after which grieving parents are encouraged to talk about anything relating to the deaths of their children. During the first two-year period following the death of a child, usually the most devastating part of the grieving process is left behind, with the parent gradually feeling less obsessed and overwhelmed by grief.

Frequently the full weight of the loss is not felt for six months, about the time friends and relatives expect parents to be recovering. At these group meetings, philosophical and religious questions are addressed, with some parents finding comfort in their faith and the firm conviction that they will see their children in an after-life. Emerson's thoughts on his deathbed were, "And now I go to find my beautiful boy." Sir William Osler's papers after his death reflected on his son who had been killed in World War I and his own imminent death when he wrote, "The Harbor almost reached after a splendid voyage and with such companions all the way, and my boy awaiting me!" Others simply try to live with their losses, but for all who participate Compassionate Friends serves an important purpose.

Regardless of the change, strife, disappointment, or calamity humans occasionally confront, we make the worst mistake by turning inward, refusing available help from the outside world. Individuals and organizations exist whose noble function is to lend a helping hand to those in need. Breaking the restraints of remaining within yourself when confronting any crisis is the first step toward converting distress to eustress, liberating yourself to return to living a productive life. A good starting point is found in taking, scoring, and heeding the results of the following Stress Inventory XIV. Properly applied, these results could make *all* the difference in improving the quality of your life.

Stress Inventory XIV
LifeScore for Your Health*

Your life style today has more to do with your tomorrows than anything else. Administer this self-checkup, scoring yourself on each item. The larger the positive score, the more the factor contributes to a healthy life. The larger the negative score, the more the factor is damaging your good health. The LifeScore computed at the end measures the total effect.

Exercise

Count the minutes per week you engage in conditioning exercise in which the heart rate (pulse) is raised to 120 beats per minute or more. Exercise sessions should last at least 15 minutes at the 120-beat level. Exercise that usually does not produce conditioning includes baseball, bowling, golf, volleyball, and slow tennis. Conditioning exercise usually comes from brisk walking, basketball, fast tennis, squash, jogging, racquetball, aerobic dancing, and other continuous, vigorous activities.

If your minutes of conditioning per week total:

Fewer than 15	Score	0	_____
15-29		+2	_____
30-44		+6	_____
45-74		+12	_____
75-119		+16	_____
120-179		+20	_____
180 or more		+24	_____

Weight

Check your weight against the weight table below. Pick your body frame size—small, medium, or large—by comparing yourself to other people of your height with different builds.
If you are overweight by:

0-5 pounds	Score	0	_____
6-15		-2	_____
16-25		-6	_____
26-35		-10	_____
36-45		-12	_____
46 or more		-15	_____

Diet

If you eat a balanced diet—one which includes, vegetables, fruits, breads, and cereals, protein foods, and dairy products:

Score   +4   _____

If you stay away from saturated fats and cholesterol, which are mostly found in animal fats:

Score   +2   _____

Smoking

If you smoke only a pipe:

Score   -4   _____

One cigar is equivalent to one cigarette. If the number of cigarettes you smoke each day is:

1-9	Score	-13	_____
10-19		-15	_____
20-29		-17	_____
30-39		-20	_____
40-49		-24	_____
50 or more		-28	_____

Extra points for women; if you smoke at all and take birth control pills:

Score   -7   _____

Alcohol

Figure the amount of alcoholic beverages you drink each day. One drink equals 1.5 ounces of liquor or 8 ounces of beer or 6 ounces of wine. If your drinks are larger, multiply accordingly.

If your average daily number of drinks totals:

0	Score	0	
1-2		+ 1	_____
3-4		- 4	_____
5-6		- 12	_____
7-9		- 20	_____
10 or more		- 30	_____

Car Accidents

If the time you wear a seat belt is:

Less than 25%	Score	0	_____
About 25%		+ 2	_____
About 50%		+ 4	_____
About 75%		+ 6	_____
About 100%		+ 8	_____

Stress

One way of measuring the stress in your life is to look at the changes in your life. The Holmes Scale (see below) is designed to do this. Add up the points for all the events on the scale that have happened to you in the past year, plus the points for all events you expect in the next year.

If your Holmes score is:

Less than 150	Score	0	_____
150-250		- 4	_____
250-300		- 7	_____
More than 300		- 10	_____

Personal History

If you have been in close contact for a year or more with someone with tuberculosis:

Score   -4   _____

If you have had radiation (x-ray) treatment of tonsils, adenoids, acne or ringworm of the scalp:

Score   -6   _____

If you work with asbestos regularly and do not smoke:

Score   -2   _____

If you work with asbestos regularly and do smoke:

Score   -10   _____

If you work regularly with vinyl chloride:

Score   -10   _____

If you live or work in a city:

Score   -6   _____

If sexual activity has been frequent and with many different partners (for potential of veneral disease):

Score   -1   _____

For women only (risk of uterine cancer); if you began regular sexual activity before age 18:

Score   -1   _____

Family History

For each parent, brother, sister who had a heart attack before age 40:

Score   -4   _____

For each grandparent, uncle, or aunt who had a heart attack before age 40:

Score   -1   _____

For each parent, brother, or sister with high blood pressure requiring treatment:

Score   -2   _____

187

For each grandparent, uncle, or aunt with high blood pressure requiring treatment:

| | Score | -1 | _____ |

For each parent, brother, or sister who got diabetes before age 25:

| | Score | -6 | _____ |

For each parent, brother, or sister who got diabetes after age 25:

| | Score | -2 | _____ |

For each grandparent, uncle, or aunt who got diabetes after age 25:

| | Score | -2 | _____ |

If you have a parent, grandparent, brother, sister, uncle, or aunt with glaucoma:

| | Score | -2 | _____ |

If you have a parent, grandparent, brother, sister, uncle, or aunt with gout:

| | Score | -1 | _____ |

For women, if your mother or sister has had cancer of the breast:

| | Score | -4 | _____ |

Medical Care

If you have had the following procedures regularly, score the points indicated:
Blood pressure check every year:

| | Score | +4 | _____ |

Self-examination of breasts monthly plus examination by physician every year or two:

| | Score | +2 | _____ |

Pap smear every year or two:

| | Score | +2 | _____ |

Tuberculosis skin test every 5 to 10 years:

        Score   +1   _____

Glaucoma test every four years after age 40:

        Score   +1   _____

Test for hidden blood in stool every two years after age 40, every year after 50:

        Score   +1   _____

Proctosigmoidoscopy once after age 50:

        Score   +1   _____

Holmes-Rahe Scale

(Check all items that happened to you in the last year or you expect in the next year.)

1.	Death of spouse	100
2.	Divorce	73
3.	Marital separation	65
4.	Jail term	63
5.	Death of close family member	63
6.	Major personal injury or illness	53
7.	Marriage	50
8.	Fired at work	47
9.	Marital reconciliation	45
10.	Retirement	45
11.	Change in health of family member	44
12.	Pregnancy	40
13.	Sex difficulties	39
14.	Gain of new family member	39
15.	Major business adjustment	39
16.	Change in financial state	38
17.	Death of close friend	37
18.	Change to different line of work	36
19.	Change in number of arguments with spouse	35
20.	Large mortgage	31
21.	Foreclosure of mortgage or loan	30
22.	Change in responsibilities of work	29

23.	Son or daughter leaving home	29
24.	Trouble with in-laws	29
25.	Outstanding personal achievement	28
26.	Spouse begins or stops work	26
27.	Start or end of formal schooling	25
28.	Change in living conditions	25
29.	Change in personal habits	24
30.	Trouble with boss	23
31.	Change in work hours or conditions	20
32.	Change in residence	20
33.	Change in schools	20
34.	Change in recreation	19
35.	Change in church activities	19
36.	Change in social activities	18
37.	Small mortgage or loan	17
38.	Change in sleeping habits	16
39.	Change in number of family get-togethers	15
40.	Change in eating habits	13
41.	Vacation*	13
42.	Christmas**	12
43.	Minor violation of the law	11

*If any **Everyone should count this.

(Of personal interest, you might return at this point to chapter three, Stress Inventory V, comparing your answers here with those given there.

Desirable Weights

Women of ages 25 and over:

Height Ft In.	Small Frame	Medium Frame	Large Frame
4 8	92-98	96-107	104-119
4 9	94-101	98-110	106-122
4 10	96-104	101-113	109-125

4 11	99-107	104-116	112-128
5 0	102-110	107-119	115-131
5 1	105-113	110-122	118-134
5 2	108-116	113-126	121-138
5 3	111-119	116-130	125-142
5 4	114-123	120-135	129-146
5 5	118-127	124-139	133-150
5 6	122-131	128-143	137-154
5 7	126-135	132-147	141-158
5 8	130-140	136-151	145-163
5 9	134-144	140-155	149-168
5 10	138-148	144-159	153-173

For women between 18 and 25, subtract 1 pound for each year under 25.

Men of ages 25 and over:

Height Ft. In.	Small Frame	Medium Frame	Large Frame
5 1	112-120	118-129	126-141
5 2	115-123	121-133	129-144
5 3	118-126	124-136	132-148
5 4	121-129	127-139	135-152
5 5	124-133	130-143	138-156
5 6	128-137	134-147	142-161
5 7	132-141	138-152	147-166
5 8	136-145	142-156	151-170
5 9	140-150	146-160	155-174
5 10	144-154	150-165	159-179
5 11	148-158	154-170	164-184
6 0	152-162	158-175	168-189
6 1	156-167	162-180	173-194
6 2	160-171	167-185	178-199
6 3	164-175	172-190	182-204

Key to your LifeScore:

Total your points:	_____
Now add:	+200
Your LifeScore:	_____

A LifeScore of 200 is above "average." If your score was above 215 you have an excellent chance of enjoying better than average health. A score of 230 or more means that odds of a healthy, long life are overwhelmingly in your favor. A score below 185 means your probability of a healthy life is decreased. Below 170 consider that you are heading for serious illness.

Another way of showing how decisions affect your health is to make a rough estimate of your life expectancy. The table below translates LifeScore to estimated life expectancy.

		Estimated Life Expectancy	
Your Health	*LifeScore*	*Men*	*Women*
Excellent	230+	81+	86+
Good	211-229	74-80	79-85
Average	191-210	67-73	72-78
Below Average	171-190	60-66	65-71
Poor	170 or less	Less than 60	Less than 65

*Vickery, Donald M. *LifePlan for Your Health*. Reading, Mass.: Addison-Wesley Publishing Company, 1977. Reprinted with permission.

**Courtesy of Metropolitan Life Insurance Company.

·10·

Living at Your Best

Which of the following two statements best illustrates the way you feel about success in life?

"It's not what you know but whom."
"It's not whom you know but what."

Many people would agree with the first statement, feeling the right contacts are far more important for success than any knowledge they might possess. Sometimes this feeling grows out of an embittered experience where we think we missed getting the job, landing the promotion, or making the sale, not because we weren't the best qualified or didn't make the best presentation, but rather because someone else had "pull." Granted these situations do arise, but even where they occur the "whom" one knows only opens the door. It doesn't guarantee success once the job has been filled or the contract signed. Performance is what counts then.

Therefore, while the "whom" may be more important initially, the "what" soon rises to the surface as the more important of the two. This is a fundamental concept which must be understood and acted on if we are to cope successfully with stress, welcoming it to help us live at our best.

A second concept, equally important has only begun to be recognized in the last two decades: there is a shift in our acceptance and understanding of what is "old" in terms of age. "Old" is a matter of perspective. Take, for instance, the example of the young teenager describing this "old" wrestler she had seen on television. When pushed to guess his age, she replied, "Oh, I'd say about thirty!"

Age is relative. Small children view teenagers as old — at least older than themselves, while some young adults might think anyone over age fifty is old. However, those who have attained age eighty and beyond don't think of themselves as old, but would likely point to centurians as old people.

With our longevity increasing and the average age of Americans rising, due in part to a lower birth rate, most of us have come to realize that age is a state of mind rather than a survival record. Harry J. Gray, chairman and chief executive officer of United Technologies Corporation, captured the essential relationship between accomplishment and age in a 1981 ad his firm ran in leading publications across America:

It's What You Do — Not When You Do It

Ted Williams, at age 42 slammed a home run in his last official time at bat.

Mickey Mantle, age 20, hit 23 home runs his first full year in the major leagues.

Golda Meir was 71 when she became prime minister of Israel.

William Pitt II was 24 when he became prime minister of Great Britain.

George Bernard Shaw was 94 when one of his plays was first produced.

Mozart was just seven when his first composition was published.

Now, how about this? Benjamin Franklin was a newspaper columnist at 16, and a framer of the United States Constitution when he was 81.

You're never too young or too old if you've got talent.

Let's recognize that just as age has little do do with ability or achievement, it also has a limited bearing on any of life's great accomplishments. What counts most in a life "well-lived" isn't longevity but the quality of life and the positive association with others, as captured in the words of the poet who wrote:

> *Man strives for glory, honor, fame,*
> *That all the world may know his name.*
> *Amasses wealth by brain and hand;*
> *Becomes a power in the land.*
> *But when he nears the end of life*
> *And looks back o'er the years of strife,*
> *He finds that happiness depends*
> *On none of these, but love of friends.*

—Anonymous

Still, many put a lot of emphasis on life expectancy. Of course, we cannot help being most interested in how long we can expect to live. Although national average life spans are

70.5 years for white males, 65.3 for all other males; 78.1 for white females, 74 for all other females, these are only averages with our curiousity aroused when considering, "Just how long will *I* live?"

Allen and Linde in their book, *Lifegain: The Exciting New Program That Will Change Your Health and Your Life,* offer another way to project individual life-expectancy. Their computations, presented below as Stress Inventory XV, are an attempt to measure longevity in relation to environment, stress, and general behavior.

━━━━━━━━━━━━━━━━━━━━━━━━━━━━━━━━━━━━━━━

Stress Inventory XV
How Long Will You Live?*

Start with the number 72.

Total
___72___

Personal Facts

If you are male, subtract 3.

If female, add 4.

If you live in an urban area with a population over 2 million, subtract 2.

If you live in a town under 10,000 or on a farm, add 2.

If any grandparent lived to 85, add 2.

If all four grandparents lived to 80, add 6.

If either parent died of a stroke or heart attack before the age of 50, subtract 4.

If any parent, brother or sister under 50 has (or had) cancer or a heart condition, or has had diabetes since childhood, subtract 3.

Do you earn over $50,000 per year? Subtract 2.

If you finished college, add 1. If you have a graduate or professional degree, add 2 more.

If you are 65 or over and still working, add 3.

If you live with a spouse or friend, add 5. If not, subtract 1 for every ten years alone since age 25.

Subtotal _____

Life Style Status

If you work behind a desk, subtract 3.

If your work requires regular, heavy physical labor, add 3.

If you exercise strenously (tennis, running, swimming, etc.) five times a week for at least a half-hour, add 4. Two or three times a week, add 2.

Do you sleep more than ten hours each night? Subtract 4.

Are you intense, aggressive, easily angered? Subtract 3.

Are you easygoing and relaxed? Add 3.

Are you happy? Add 1. Unhappy? Subtract 2.

Have you had a speeding ticket in the past year? Subtract 1.

Do you smoke more than two packs a day? Subtract 8. One to two packs? Subtract 6. One-half to one? Subtract 3.

Do you drink the equivalent of 1.5 oz. of liquor a day? Subtract 1.

Are you overweight by 50 pounds or more? Subtract 8. By 30 to 50 pounds? Subtract 4. By 10 to 30 pounds? Subtract 2.

If you are a man over 40 and have annual checkups, add 2.

If you are a woman and see a gynecologist once a year, add 2.
Subtotal _____

Age Adjustment

If you are between 30 and 40, add 2.

If you are between 40 and 50, add 3.

If you are between 50 and 70, add 4.

If you are over 70, add 5.
Subtotal _____

Total subtotals for your life expectancy score _____

*Allen, Robert F. and Linde, Shirley. *Lifegain: The Exciting New Program That Will Change Your Health and Your Life.* New York: Appleton-Century-Crofts Books, 1981.

Years ago a Wyoming rancher explained, "There are two things we must do in life: one is to pay taxes, the other is to die, but there are a few things we *ought* to do in between." Following and applying the seven principles below in our daily living is one of the best ways to fulfill those "few" things we *ought* to do in between being born, paying taxes, and dying. While there is no guarantee of success, applying these will enable you to realize better the goal of this book, to "Welcome stress! It can help you be your best!"

The "IZE" Have It

If you want stress to work *for* rather than *against* you, you must adhere closely to the following seven "IZE."

1. *Memorize:* Each day you should make a concentrated effort to memorize one great truth. These might include:

"They can who think they can." —Virgil

"All that I have seen teaches me to trust the Creator for all that I have not seen." —Emerson

"Attitude is always more important than fact." —Dr. Karl Menninger

"Whether you think you can or can't, you're right." —Henry Ford

"Anything man's mind can conceive and believe, man can achieve." —Napoleon Hill

"The larger the island of knowledge, the longer the shoreline of wonder." —Dr. Ralph Sockman

"It is our attitude at the beginning of a difficult undertaking which, more than anything else, will determine its successful outcome." —Dr. William James

"The Lord is my Shepherd, I shall not want..."
—Psalm 23

"I'd rather be the man who bought the Brooklyn Bridge than the man who sold it." —Will Rogers

"A man cannot directly choose his circumstances, but he can choose his thoughts and so indirectly, yet surely, shape his circumstances." —James Allen

An easy way to memorize one great truth each day is to type it on a 3" x 5" card, carry it in your pocket or purse, and read it whenever a free moment occurs in your day. By concentrating daily on one great thought and working it into both the conscious and subconscious memory bank, you will have ready access to truths from great minds which will be invaluable in helping you channel stress into eustress. These memorable lines can be found in the Bible or culled from other reading, especially biographies of great people, or from newspapers, inspirational books and magazines, or any number of sources readily available in any public library.

Memorization can be made easier by using cassette tapes, playing inspirational, motivational, and/or educational tapes daily. Remember that the mind must be exposed to material at least six times before it begins to penetrate the memory bank and lodge at the subconscious level. Obviously some material will take longer, but through spaced repetition—listening to the same information repeatedly over a period of time—learning takes place. The material is memorized and can be recalled.

What you have stored in your memory bank in large part determines whether your whole thought structure is positive or negative. The following Stress Inventory XVI will help you assess your current orientation, whether positive toward success and eustress or negative toward failure and distress.

Stress Inventory XVI
Which Side Do You Choose?*

Read the lists below. Circle those characteristics which apply to you. The column which has the most circles probably indicates your general direction in life.

After you have read this chapter, apply the principles learned to resolve or change those behaviors and attitudes which you circled in the Failure column.

The 10 Commandments for Success

1. Persistence
2. Good attitude
3. Imagination
4. Desire
5. Belief in truth and self
6. Determination
7. Enthusiasm
8. Practice
9. Development or growth
10. Self-motivation

The 13 Commandments for Failure

1. Worry
2. Doubt
3. Fear
4. Self-pity
5. Can't-do-it
6. Put-it-off
7. Complain
8. Hate
9. Indecisive
10. Dreamer/wisher
11. Run yourself down
12. Cheater
13. Quitter

*Adapted from Arnold "Nick" Carter, *The Amazing Results—Full World of Cassette Learning!* Chicago: Nightingale-Conant Corp., 1980, p. 29.

The ability to use our minds whether to memorize, recall material we've learned, or remember the past is a real asset. However, those who are suffering grievous losses may wonder whether the memory is an asset or a liability. For instance, experiencing the death of someone such as a spouse is one of life's greatest shocks. Mentally wrestling with the suddenness of the loss is almost overwhelming. At this point, the memory seems a curse rather than a blessing. For the widow, her husband's former place at the table is conspicuously vacant. When doing the laundry, she becomes acutely aware that when he took off those clothes, little did either of them know he'd never wear them again. Then there's the shed left partly painted and the axe left wedged in the stump at the woodpile. In moments of desperation, she wonders whether she wouldn't be better off never having known him. Yet, as time dulls the pain, those who are left know that they'd never really give up the memories of pleasant, comfortable, loving times in the past.

The old entertainer, Ted Lewis, summed up the importance of memory when he responded to a young man's inquiry,

Son, you ask me what I have in my old age,
To show for all the years I spent on the stage?
Boy, I've got a million memories locked way down here,
And I can write my check on them any day
of the year.

Among all the assets of memory, perhaps the most prized is the way we are able to make transitions to more difficult periods of life, reliving better days, thereby easing the turbulence when making undesirable adjustments.

2. *Crystallize:* When Alice in Wonderland came to a crossroad while walking in the woods she hesitated, inquir-

ing of the Cheshire Cat: "Would you tell me please, which way I ought to walk from here?"

"That depends a good deal on where you want to get to," said the Cat.

"I don't much care where..." said Alice.

"Then it doesn't matter which way you walk," replied the Cat.

We can compare our own approach to life to Alice's attitude. We may have vague long-range goals, but no immediate plans whatsoever as to how to achieve them. It is impossible to reach any destination, execute any approach, or fulfill any purpose, without a plan or a series of mini-plans leading to the main objective, unless the goal is achieved by chance.

If a traveler were to approach a ticket counter in a major airport exclaiming, "Sell me a ticket," the agent would be certain to inquire, "Where do you want to go?" If the would-be traveler responded, "I really don't know," the trip would be over before it started.

Such an approach to life would be similar to a loose cannon on deck and potentially just as dangerous.

In achieving goals we must deal with both short-term and long-term objectives, for any major goal is comprised of many little goals. If you are in sales and want to sell "X" number of units this year, this annual sales volume must be broken down into monthly, weekly, and daily quotas, but even here the goals would not be specific enough. To sell "Y" number of units each day—and daily goals at times exceed while at others fall short of the mark—you know you must make "Z" number of presentations, which requires contacting a certain number of prospects, either in person or by phone.

It seems quite simple and, as is usually the case, this plan is easy to follow *but only if it is worked.* To be effective, goals must be crystallized, i.e., reduced to their smallest parts. Once this is done, these parts fit as in a mosaic, combining to project beauty that can only be observed once each small part is in place. A prime example is noted in Fulton Oursler's *Modern Parables*. A certain man fell upon hard times in a business venture many years ago. He had run the business honestly so that none of his investors could complain when it failed with indebtedness of $300,000 and they had to settle at twenty-seven cents on each dollar invested.

Facing the world again, Reuben entered the advertising business. Laboring day and night, through the years he became successful. His new venture filled a need providing the public with a new service, so that by middle age he was a wealthy, though unhappy man. This led him to his secret quest. Investigators were sent out with instructions to hunt down his creditors from twenty-two years earlier who had accepted only partial settlement on their investment. There were many of them, by now located throughout the country. Where deaths had occurred heirs were found, one a scrub-woman in the Chicago City Hall.

On New Year's Day, 1927, Reuben sat at his library desk, writing the first check for $10,000 to the scrubwoman. Working throughout the afternoon with a stack of blank checks and a list of names and addresses, he mailed checks that day totaling $645,000, paying 100 cents on the dollar, and interest as well, on debts which by law no longer existed.

Everyone is familiar with Reuben's name for, in full, it is Reuben H. Donnelley, founder of the company which prints the Classified Telephone Directory, telephone books in which one is listed by business or profession. By crystallizing his goal to do right by those who had placed their trust in him, Donnelley was a far happier man in later years.

Another virtue in crystallizing goals, plans, and objectives, is that it helps us maintain a proper perspective, approaching life on a day-to-day basis. For instance, it is easy to make a case for doom and gloom considering only scant facts in many daily newspapers. Yet, many good things occur each day in all communities. In fact, good far outweighs evil nearly everywhere, which causes a shortage of "bad news." The media's emphasis on the negative is actually a positive sign, for the one factor in any report making it newsworthy is that it is different or unusual.

Thefts are newsworthy because most people are honest. Accidents receive ample coverage precisely because most people travel to and from their destinations without mishap. Murders are emblazoned across headlines because most people respect the sanctity of life. Rapes are newsworthy because most males aren't so blatantly hostile as to attack females. These negative incidents are the *exceptions* rather than the rule, which make them newsworthy. Of course good items are carried in nearly all publications, but it is obvious that news (the exceptions) will predominate over good reports (the usual) for publishers and broadcasters.

Aside from reading daily newspapers and listening to radio news reports while driving or watching the evening news in vibrant color, comfortably seated in our living rooms, we need to place emphasis on the positive, for if limited solely to news, our minds will be saturated with the negative. Never lose sight of the other side of the coin: *the positive far outweighs the negative nearly everywhere we turn.* If you have any momentary doubts of this, study your own community in the past twenty-four hours. Were most people molested in your town? Were the majority of adolescents in school or out until all hours of the evening committing acts of vandalism? Were most family members apparently concerned with the safety of one another, or were most wives mad enough to kill because of their mates' physical abuse during the night?

When considering the moral state of the country, it would be easy to assume the nation is not as stable as it was earlier in history because churches do not exert the same influence as in previous decades. Yet, church attendance is only one variable which needs to be weighed against a backdrop of many other factors which George Gallup, Jr., executive director of the Princeton Religion Research Center explained in a recent Associated Press story. His research reflected an overwhelming belief in God by Americans. He further found that most Americans pray regularly; nearly half attend church each Sunday, and almost every American home in the United States has at least one Bible, though it may also be the least read book in the home! All of this attests to a "remarkable stability of religion in America," Gallup noted.

This perspective is lost on those who focus only on negative conclusions from the same study, including widespread biblical illiteracy, prayers usually focusing on requests rather than thanksgiving, with some Americans viewing God as a "divine Santa Claus." Furthermore, according to the same pollster, Americans have a higher degree of confidence in organized religion than in any other of the ten major institutions in society, which include government, banking, the news media, business, education, and the military. Seeing the forest is sometimes necessary before we can appreciate the tree.

3. *Specialize:* One sure way to get an edge on competitors in any field is to specialize. Specializing makes for uniqueness which causes one to stand out in an enviable way. Of course, becoming a specialist requires that we accept the challenge of daring to be different.

One of the ironies of modern life is that the more specialized we become on one subject, the more the public is likely to credit our opinions on any subject. A prime example in the last decade was a pediatrician identified in the public eye as an expert on foreign affairs, a reputation gained largely from his identification as a well-known physician! Theologians are frequently asked their opinions on a myriad of subjects unrelated to their field, and entertainers influence our political decisions. Everyone is entitled to his or her opinion, but those who have become specialists in the public eye have a particular obligation to avoid holding themselves out as experts in fields other than the ones in which they have acquired expertise.

A fact often overlooked is that the more education or training received in a specific field, the more narrow the focus of specialty becomes. For instance, an undergraduate degree may be a broad study of diverse fields, but all graduate degrees are designed to train specialists who will know a great deal about one small segment in a particular field of study.

Everyone can become a specialist in a sense, even if their work doesn't fit the descriptions above, for anyone who consistently tries hard and makes his or her best effort will surely be distinguished. However, the problem in motivating people to become workers and achievers begins long before they reach responsible positions in the adult working world. Parents from time immemorial have had to face the issue, "How do we inspire our children to live up to their best when the natural tendency is to identify with the crowd, avoiding the challenge to be different?" Sometimes this problem grows out of parents' constant dream and admonition that their children do better in life than they have. This may not be an entirely selfless issue, as obviously the success of children reflects favorably on their parents, but aside from this potentially ulterior motive, should we be content to let a child be "average" when he or she is capable of much more?

And just what is average? In this case it means being less than your best, making a half-hearted rather than whole-hearted effort in whatever you choose to do. To be average is the lazy person's escape, a cop-out. It is living by default, taking the easiest way out, not preparing to make those contributions in life that are possible, but mostly trying to ignore them so the conscience can exist in ease, if not luxury. Being content to get by or to try for nothing more than what is average is to occupy space without purpose or to take life's trip without paying the fare. Recipients of such a "free ride" never recognize that service to others is the only rent we pay for our space here on earth. One content with being average will never be equipped to be of any *real* service to others or even to himself.

The average person passes life away with time, rather than passing time away with life. For the average person, time is something to be killed rather than worked, with satisfaction achieved at the end of the trail approximately equal to the investment made while on the journey. Successful people, on the other hand, who strive to make their best effort are remembered for their contributions to life. Even those who never reach great heights are at least remembered because they tried.

Hopefully these ideas will trigger internal desires for you to improve yourself in your own area of work, whether in business, a profession, or the home. "Doing your best," and "giving your all" have fringe benefits as well. Your self-concept will improve. Also, a sense of job security will be afforded which is not felt by those who have been content to remain undistinguished.

Some people would complain that there is not time to go the extra mile, but there *is* if we will begin filtering sound principles of time management into our daily lives. First is the need for establishing priorities. Stop for a few moments each evening making a list of all the things you hope to accomplish the following day. Once the list is made, order your priorities by ranking them according to the importance of each task. Some tasks will fall into the "must" category, others can be assigned to "things I should do," though still others can be listed as "not important." Assign each item to one of these three categories, recognizing that all tasks in anyone's day are not of equal worth. Avoid procrastination, tackling items in the "must" category at the first opportunity the following morning.

Experts in the field of time management inform us that paperwork crossing our desks at work or at home should be handled but once. Most decisions concerning important mail can be decided on and acted on immediately. Interruptions waste more productive time than perhaps any other cause. Establish a schedule where others know you are not to be disturbed except in cases of emergencies. Fellow office workers or neighbors will respect your scheduling and with your taking charge, far more will be accomplished each day.

To focus your efforts and maximize your potential, assess your strengths and weaknesses. Be both frank and honest as you view yourself realistically in Stress Inventory XVII.

Stress Inventory XVII
Measuring Strengths and Weaknesses[*]

Assess your strengths and weaknesses as honestly and as objectively as possible. Concentrate on seeing yourself as you think others see you. This image forms a significant part of your self-concept and, consequently, is most important in determining the best area in which to consider specializing.

1. What are the 3 greatest strengths you bring to your work?
   (1) _____
   (2) _____
   (3) _____

2. What do you consider your 3 greatest strengths in your personal life outside your work?
   (1) _____
   (2) _____
   (3) _____

3. Quickly, list your 3 greatest weaknesses:
   (1) _____
   (2) _____
   (3) _____

4. How many of your greatest strengths listed above do you regularly use in your job? How are these used?
   (1) _____
   (2) _____
   (3) _____

5. How are your greatest weaknesses exposed in your work?
   (1) _____
   (2) _____
   (3) _____

6. List 3 things you like most about your job.
   (1) _____
   (2) _____
   (3) _____

7. List 3 things you least like about your job.
   (1) _____
   (2) _____
   (3) _____

8. With this self-appraisal of your work-related strengths and
   weaknesses, in which area of specialization would you be best
   suited? Why?

   _____
   _____
   _____

*Adapted from McManus and Clarke's *Life Stress Profile: A Projective
Technique,* Medical City Dallas, #250, Dallas, TX 75230.

4. *Neutralize:* If we are to succeed in directing stress into eustress so that we learn to welcome stress, we must neutralize our fears, eliminating the cause of so much of our distress. One of the greatest fears of most Americans today is the fear of serious illness such as cancer. In *Anatomy of an Illness,* which relates his victory over a painful disease, Norman Cousins brilliantly makes the case that if people can be programmed to die, they can be programmed to live. Thus, in order to neutralize our fear of death, we must concentrate on our own participation in programming ourselves to live.

In recent years far more responsibility for patient survival has been placed on medical professionals than is warranted. In spite of numerous exciting advances in the medical field, attitude and determination of the patient remain the chief factors preventing premature death. Where patients *expect* to get well, cure rates exceed medical expectations; similarly, when patients "know" they are going to die, the death rate is far higher than might be medically expected. This suggests that mind power deserves far more credit than it is usually given.

Every ounce of our strength opposes death. It's a loser, a downer, the opposite of all we desire. "Born to live," we ask ourselves, "we die to what?" No one knows what lies beyond the Great Divide separating us from loved ones no longer here. Seeing a wife's or mother's body artificially prepared for viewing will suggest the thought: *but where did she go?*

The late Cecil B. DeMille while drifting in a small boat one day observed a water beetle as it crawled up the side of his craft from the water, settling on the boat's rim where the sun baked it in its cocoon. For the next several hours DeMille drifted about, planning an upcoming screen venture, giving no thought to the dried cocoon or the water beetle. Later, noticing a small break in the side of the cocoon, he was amazed when a magnificent dragon fly emerged. Hesitating for a moment as if not wanting to leave familiar surroundings, in an instant it flew off as if it had always known how to fly. It flew high above the water and then down close to the water's surface. Water beetles on the bottom of the lake could have observed their former kind in its new existence if only they could have seen well enough and looked up. In a moment, the dragon fly with scintillating colors flashing on its wings soared further than a water beetle could travel over an entire lifespan. DeMille concluded, "If God in His wisdom will do this for the water beetle, think what He must hold in store for man!"

Our minds will probably never rest until the last word on death has been discovered, for the mind always questions, probes, and explores. Yet, intellectually man need not be restricted by the confines of his physical world. Clearly DeMille shared a noble concept with us worthy of our reflection, as we examine life as but a way-station on the journey toward becoming.

Several years ago, Jessica Mitford in *American Way of Death* decried practices that detracted from the family's dignity when faced with the death of a family member. She observed that in our attempts to deny death, we do not afford the family the opportunity of a therapeutic grief response. Sometimes, in our haste to neutralize or filter out all negatives from life, we are guilty of throwing out the curd with the whey.

However, neutralizing negatives is confined not only to bad health or facing grief over the loss of a loved one. Other stress-producing situations influence us daily which must be changed if we are to avoid acute distress. One of these is noise, stressful because of (1) its psychological impact where the noise is unwanted or distracting, and (2) its physical disturbance of volume and/or frequency. Noise is sound which involves vibrations and mechanical waves. The loudness of the noise is measured in decibels (dB) by the powers of ten. Hence an increase of 0 to 10 dB represents sound 10 times as great; increases from 10 to 20 dB represents sounds 100 times as great, as sound intensity multiplies by ten with every 10 dB increase.

Human hearing ranges from 0 dB (no sound) to beyond 150 dB, at which level intense pain occurs. Following are the effects of some noise levels:

dB Level	Effect
140+	An acute exposure; may damage hearing
130	Pain threshold
70	Potential hearing loss begins
65	Evidence of stress response begins
40	Sleep disrupted
0	Hearing begins

Research studies show that chronic exposure to excess noise can cause increased heart rate and blood pressure, degenerative hearing processes, decreased learning ability, increased error rate even in simple tasks, and a decrease in one's ability to concentrate or to perform analytical functions. A decrease in short-term memory has also been found to result from excess noise and—what is most alarming to industry—an increased accident rate attributed to constant excessive job noise.

Review the list below for the decibel levels of common sounds in your daily life. How many are you exposed to each day and for how long?

Sounds	*Average dB*
Police siren at 100 feet	135
Pneumatic (air) drill at 5 feet	125
Inside discotheque	125
Inside boiler room	110
Chain saw at 30 feet	100
Riveting gun at 25 feet	100
Gasoline mower	90
City traffic at 5 feet	90
Inside a stenographic room	75
Electric shaver	75
Vacuum cleaner	75
Average residential street	55
Refrigerator	40
Quiet office	40
Library	38
Soft whisper at 15 feet	25
Hearing begins	0

Interestingly, our environment is seldom totally devoid of sound, as noted with a 38 decibel level even in a library. Some sounds can be more easily avoided than others, such as the 125 decibel level in a discotheque. Noises on the job are not so easily avoidable. However, it is in the best interest of workers and industry to reduce job noise levels as much as possible.

If job noise continually causes stress, keeping the individual anxious and tense, ways should be explored to reduce either (1) the noise level or (2) seek a job transfer where there is less noise. Rotation of workers is another possible way of neutralizing work stress caused by noise fatigue.

In general, humor is one of the best methods of neutralizing and controlling distress, especially when we laugh at our own follies. A golfer who played incredibly poorly was out on the course one day where he shot an exceptional 84; not bad until we learn this was on the front nine! As he teed off toward the tenth hole, he sliced his shot. Frustration turned to rage as he bent his number one wood into a V-shape over his knee, using profanity that could have barred him from any course.

Still livid with anger, he looked about for another source at which he could vent his feelings, spotting his hapless caddy standing off to one side. Addressing him he said, "And you have to be the world's worst caddy!" to which his caddy replied, "Oh, no sir, that would be entirely too much of a coincidence."

An ability to laugh and not take ourselves too seriously is helpful in neutralizing and controlling stress that can easily become distress.

5. *Minimize:* There are those who can find difficulties in their opportunities, just as readily as others discover opportunities in their difficulties. Many times it depends on our perspective, i.e., the way we view ourselves compared to the way we see others. However, all too often we are comparing our weaknesses with others' perceived strengths. This is how we fall into the trap of assuming others' marriages are far better than ours, for after all, in our homes we know what our mates look like in the morning without benefit of razors, hairdryers, after-shave, or makeup.

Similarly, when glancing at another's job, we are too busy admiring the froth to be aware of the dregs of boredom arising from repetition found in any work. Hence we come off second-best, primarily because of an unrealistic comparison at the outset.

Most of us would do well to minimize our failures and maximize our successes. We do this all the time when appraising others. For instance, Babe Ruth is recognized internationally as the home-run king of baseball. Another fact often overlooked—though probably never forgotten by the Bambino himself—was that he also held the distinction of being the strike-out king of the world's number one sport, having struck out more times at bat than any other player! Had Babe Ruth not possessed the ability to minimize his failures, undoubtedly he would never have succeeded in becoming the home-run king. Of such strength come winners in all walks of life!

Art Linkletter is another who minimizes difficulties in his life, looking back on missed opportunities without rancor. He related this story in a 1981 interview with *Success* magazine. Several years ago he was approached by Walt Disney, and together they rode some twenty-five miles outside the city of Los Angeles. Stopping the car at a spot where there was nothing but open space, the two got out and walked around while Walt described to Art his dream of establishing an amusement park on this site, one that would appeal to children of all ages from three to ninety-three. He concluded describing his dream by telling Art that he didn't need any more capital investment for the project, but that he had no money left to buy up any of the surrounding land. "So," he said, "as a good friend I wanted to give you the first opportunity at buying up land next to this amusement park, land which is going to become invaluable in just a few years."

Art said as he looked around, all he could see was blowing sand, a scraggy tree here and there and miles to go before returning to civilization. As they walked back to the car talking it over, Art made his decision telling Walt as they reached the car, "I have my money tied up in other investments, and I think I'll just let this one pass." Of course the amusement park became the fabulously successful Disneyland, with the adjoining property worth literally millions today. Is Art Linkletter bitter? All he laughingly says is, "Looking back, I figure as I evaluated that opportunity while returning to the car parked in that wasteland that afternoon, every step I took cost me a million dollars!" Even when viewing some of life's most perplexing problems, many times what is of utmost importance is our assessment of the difficulty. Every experience in life can make you better or bitter—the choice is yours.

6. *Maximize:* Just as we need to minimize our liabilities we must maximize our assets. For many this is difficult as we are much more likely to be aware of our failures than successes, as discussed earlier. Controlling those thoughts we permit to enter the mind is where the battle is fought to determine if we are going to enjoy maximum growth leading to greater contentment and fulfillment. This is where someone suggests, "But aren't you talking about 'Positive Thinking' and isn't that just an easy out?" Granted, at first glance the suggestion that positive thinking can make a difference appears simplistic; yet, nothing could be further from the truth.

Similarly, when we hear "It's too good to be true," we think of something that far exceeded someone's level of expectations. However, when something is truly good, it just is not possible for it to be *too* good to be true.

It has long been considered sport to try to put down those who admonish us to "think positively." We have been told that as a solution to problems such an answer is too easy. This argument misses the point: the value of a positive mental attitude comes when *approaching* a task. To think positively is *not a solution* to problems, yet it is probably the most important mental framework when considering solutions. Becoming involved in possibility thinking means that alternatives and solutions are considered more deeply and creatively.

Far more worrisome, however, is the criticism that to think positively is an easy approach to life's problems. Nothing is more patently false. It is far more difficult to be positive than negative. We are constantly tempted to approach problems in a negative manner. Our assumptions are based upon what will *not* work rather than considering what *will* work. This latter is where a positive mental attitude sets the stage for possibility thinking, but first we must overcome the handicap of "it can't be done," or "it's never been done that way before." Actually a new approach may be the solution simply *because* it's never been done that way before.

A positive mental attitude permits the individual to approach problems from a perspective that considers all options. When we discipline ourselves sufficiently so that we look beyond an instinctive negative rejection of our options, then we are living life at a depth which eludes most people.

Possibility thinking requires great mental effort, but negatives can be turned into positives in almost every instance. A small businessman owned a little dry-goods building in the middle of a huge square block that was fast being bought up by a merchandising giant. When approached, the businessman refused to sell. "Don't you realize," he was asked, "now that we have bought all sites in this block except yours, when we build our new mammoth store we will drive you out of business?" Still, the small businessman remained adamant and undeterred. Month after month he watched as construction proceeded with the huge store, as promised, encircling his small store in the middle of the block. Finally, when the grand opening day arrived for the new dry goods department store, banners were unfurled along the front of the building proclaiming, "GRAND OPENING." The small businessman had his banner in place over his door with letters of equal size advising the public, "MAIN ENTRANCE"! This is an example of turning lemons into lemonade, which is usually the secret behind any success story, individually or corporately.

Sometimes we become overwhelmed by the negatives. Each year crime statistics are up with reports that Americans are living in greater fear than ever. Man's inhumanity to others seems to outweigh by far whatever good is out there in a heartless, cruel world. Yet, looking for the good in life challenges us to live better ourselves, with a ripple effect spreading further than anything we might imagine. But first, we need to note the positive which begs for our attention just as does the less desirable. For instance, consider the following recent good news stories:

• Blind Nathaniel Lewis, 79, of Dallas, Texas, was robbed of his total savings of $217.00. Following the robbery he said, "I just want to die." With the spread of his story, offers to help poured in, with his money restored several times over. Asked what he now thinks of this old world, he replied, "The world ain't so bad." And so it isn't!

• In San Diego, California, Scoutmaster Sidney Loman had over 9,000 boys move through his Bethel A.M.E. Church scout troop since he first organized it in 1921. Both his legs were amputated, so that he conducted weekly scout meetings from his wheelchair. Loman always advised his boys, "First, be obedient to God, then to man." Nodding to the American flag, he would add, "The red is for bravery, the white is for a clean heart, clean hands and a clean mind, and the blue is for 'true blue' to God and to man." It should be noted that Scoutmaster Loman was 100 years old when he died, the world's oldest scoutmaster actively continuing to influence positively the lives of young boys.

• In Portsmouth, Virginia, a posse of 100 women and children chased a suspected exhibitionist, corralling him for police. Seen trying to break into a house in a neighborhood that had been disrupted by a man fitting his description who had exposed himself, a sixteen-year-old girl armed with a lead pole and wearing only a nightgown led the group. The suspect told police, "I'm glad you're here. I thought they were going to kill me." So much for others always refusing to get involved!

• After eleven-year-old Morgan Rowe of Gainsville, Florida, lost his left arm in an accident, he spent five years selling bottles and newspapers to raise money to pay off his medical bills. With help from strangers who heard of his efforts, he was able to pay off his $30,000 medical bill. "I thought I'd be grown before I paid it off," said a jubilant Rowe, who obviously knows something about individual initiative at a very young age.

One sector of our population—the elderly—often see themselves as helpless in the face of neighborhood crime. Yet, even here, senior citizens are not without opportunity to seize the initiative and keep crime on the run in their own neighborhoods. Among the most successful efforts, according to law-enforcement officials, are the formal crime-prevention programs.

Formal crime-prevention programs offer assistance to an increasing number of neighborhood-watch or block-security groups in local communities. In neighborhoods where these programs have been put into effect, crime has been substantially reduced. Getting people involved is important to the success of these programs, bringing credit to participating individuals and the neighborhoods they serve. These programs take many forms. In one neighborhood all residents were given bumper stickers, identifying cars as belonging to those living in the community. People were then asked to watch for cars in the neighborhood which did not display these decals, writing down license numbers for later use should anything be discovered awry.

Closer neighbor ties have resulted in several of the communities where the neighborhood watches have begun. Neighbors feel the community has been returned to them, that they have a vital part in making certain the community remains safe, and citizens appreciate the security discovered in standing together to deliver a fatal blow to those who would prey on the weak, the alone, or the elderly. One resident where such a program has been instituted stated, "The biggest thing is that we're watching out for each other." This is an important concept of neighborhood integrity which has too long been ignored. All available policemen in a community are not as effective at *preventing* crime as a well-organized citizens' group where people take their crime-prevention roles seriously. Though good police forces are absolutely essential in any community, policemen will be the first to agree that prevention is an aspect of crime control which can only be effectively carried out by society at large. This is where neighborhood-watch or block-security groups enter the scene.

Sometimes such a program only comes about as a response to crime. As long as community residents feel "It can't happen to me," it is impossible to get the necessary numbers of people involved to make such a program work effectively. In all too many instances such groups have been formed only after several robberies have convinced neighbors, "It can *too* happen to me!"

However, beyond the mechanics of these worthwhile programs, I suspect they also do much psychological good for those involved. No longer do involved residents feel helpless; they are *not*. No longer do they feel alone in their concern. Knowing others are involved is needed reassurance. Fear is lessened because there is always safety and comfort in numbers.

In some elderly neighborhoods, block patrols have been formed. Unarmed, these patrols are visible on the street during the day, many with transmitters tuned to a frequency where help can be summoned immediately if necessary. Such programs have freed the elderly from living fearfully behind locked doors, opening not only the streets, but also the parks to the law-abiding people who are primarily responsible for the upkeep of such community projects in the first place.

Senior citizens interested in forming such neighborhood-watch or block-security groups should contact their local police departments, who will be happy to lend the needed assistance in getting such programs underway. Beneficiaries are not only neighborhood residents and local police departments, but by reducing crime the whole community reaps both measurable and immeasurable benefits. Speaking of maximizing strengths and using talents wisely, older citizens are a large pool of untapped resources available for any community willing to organize and draw on both their experience and wisdom.

7. *Recognize:* Finally, it is imperative that every individual recognize that there is not only some good within each of us, but that in most cases the good far outweighs the bad, regardless of past mistakes. Recognizing the need of forgiving the *self* first enables one to be more open and forgiving

of others, eliminating grudges and hatred which have poisoned the mind.

At a sales convention a woman speaker, Marsha, stood on stage telling her story. She had grown up on a farm in the East and, as far back as she could remember, her mother had been dying from cancer. For the last few years of her life the mother was bedridden. Each morning she would say to her husband as he started out to tend to farm chores, "Darling, I would feel so much better if only this room were painted blue." Marsha said, "My father would always reply, 'You know how busy I am today with all that needs my attention on the place, but soon I'm going to buy some beautiful blue paint just like you want for the walls of this room.'"

One day in her early teens, Marsha awakened to discover her mother had died during the night. "That afternoon," she said, "my father went into town, bought a gallon of blue paint, came home and began painting that bedroom blue." In describing the anger and resentment coursing through her body, she told how she sat on the sofa in the living room while her father painted, wondering why he had been so cruel? Why hadn't he taken the time to paint the room when it would have meant something to her mother? The more she thought of this the angrier she grew until something snapped within and, recognizing a great truth which occasionally confronts each of us in a dramatic way, Marsha concluded, "Right then and there I decided to learn something from this experience that would benefit others so long as I lived, for I resolved never again to let a single day pass in my life where I failed to 'paint at least one room blue' for someone else."

This is the recognition that enables us to approach stress directly in our lives, welcoming it, sifting through it for those valuable lessons contained within, and then applying what we've learned to channel stress away from distress toward eustress so that going to work, coming home, or just relaxing for a day becomes a joy.

It is easy and natural to devote energy to those things we do well; most people are attracted to those tasks they perform best. If we are not careful, though, an inordinate amount of our energy is consumed in narrow pursuits.

Most of all, we need to remain aware of the advice, "Man can accomplish just about any amount of work as long as it isn't the work he is *supposed* to be doing at this time."

Is there a prescription for better living? Yes! Begin today to live life at its best, recognizing that a balanced life is necessary for sound mental health; that there is a time for work, a time for play, a time for rest, and a time for involvement, and that there is no virtue in extremism, with "moderation in all things" as sound advice today as when first recorded some 2,000 years ago.

A man who was approaching the winter of his life remarked, "If I had life to live over, I'd pick more daisies." He would sit back and do nothing more often, go on more picnics, go barefoot earlier in the spring and later in the fall. He would take time to be sillier in another life, would be less hygienic, take both more chances and more trips. He would eat more ice cream and less bran, experience more actual troubles and fewer imaginary ones. He would play hockey more, have more sweethearts, keep later hours, and go to more circuses. In a word, he would *enjoy* life more had he the opportunity to live it over.

Most importantly for all of us, life has its moments to be savored. Everyone experiences mountaintop moments, but most people would probably agree there are too few. Resolving to live in the present, appreciating the moments at hand today will enable us to deposit fond memories in our memory banks and strengthen us for whatever stress the future may hold.

Now, for a final exercise in welcoming stress, apply the instructions contained in Stress Inventory XVIII. In a very short time you will discover the inherent truth in the challenging title of this book, *Welcome Stress! It Can Help You Be Your Best.*

Stress Inventory XVIII
The "IZE" Have It

Starting with the first day of the week, go back and read the section on the first of the seven "IZE" discussed in this chapter. Throughout the day, seek every opportunity to apply this concept in your life. Keep a record by placing a check in the appropriate column each time you have successfully applied the concept during that day. Each day center your attention on another of the seven concepts. Repeat this task for six weeks. You will be on the road to new behavior and far greater fulfillment in your life!

	Sun.	Mon.	Tues.	Wed.	Thurs.	Fri.	Sat.
1. Memorize							
2. Crystallize							
3. Specialize							
4. Neutralize							
5. Minimize							
6. Maximize							
7. Recognize							

References

Chapter Two

1. *Teen-Aged Pregnancy, the Problem That Hasn't Gone Away,* (New York: Alan Guttmacher Institute, 1981), pp. 11ff.
2. Levitas, Irving M., *You Can Beat the Odds on Heart Attack,* (Indianapolis: Bobbs-Merrill Co., Inc., 1975), p. 45.
3. J. Brown, *et. al.,* "Nutritional and Epidemiologic Factors Related to Heart Disease," *World Review of Nutrition and Dietetics,* 1970, vol. 12.

Chapter Three

1. Culligan, Matthew J. and Sedlack, Keith, *How to Avoid Stress Before It Kills You,* (New York: Grammercy Publishing Co., 1976).

Chapter Seven

1. Hegarty, Christopher J., "Do You Work Too Hard? An Expert Explains the Dangers," *U.S. News and World Report,* March 26, 1979.
2. "Stress: How It Can Hurt," *Newsweek,* April 21, 1980.

Bibliography

Allen, James. *As A Man Thinketh.* Westwood, New Jersey: Fleming H. Revell Company, 1976.

Allen, Robert F. and Linde, Shirley. *Lifegain: The Exciting New Program That Will Change Your Health and Your Life.* New York: Appleton-Century-Crofts Books, 1981.

American Association of Marriage and Family Therapists. "Alcoholic in the Family?", Claremont, California, 1977.

Anderson, H., *et. al.,* "Executives Under Stress." *Newsweek* (August 24, 1981) 98:53.

Baldwin, Bruce A. "Professional Burnout: Occupational Hazard and Preventable Problem." *Pace,* Vol. 8, No. 1, January/February, 1981, p. 20ff.

Bane, Mary Jo and Masnick, George. *The Nation's Families: 1960-1990.* Boston: Auburn House Publishing Company, 1980.

Basile, Frank. *Come Fly with Me.* Indianapolis: Charisma Publications, Inc., 1978. ("The Guy in the Glass," Dale Wimbrow.)

Bennett, The Honorable Charles E. Testifying in a hearing before the Subcommittee on Elementary, Secondary, and Vocational Education of the House Committee on Education and Labor, April 24, 1979.

Benson, H. *The Relaxation Response.* New York: William Morrow and Company, 1975.

Berland, Theodore. *Diets '81.* Skokie, Illinois: Consumer Guide, 1981.

Breslow, Lester. "Risk Factor Intervention for Health Maintenance." *Science* (May 26, 1978) 200:908-12.

Breslow, Lester and Enstrom, James E. "Persistence of Health Habits and Their Relationship to Mortality." *Preventive Medicine* (July 1, 1980) 9:4, 469-483.

Brown, J.; Bourke, C.J.; Gearity, G.F.; Finnegan, A.; Hill, M.; Heffernan-Fox, S.C.; Fitzgerald, D.E.; Kennedy, J.; Childers, R.W.; Jessop, W.J.E.; Trulson, M.F.; Latham, M.C.; Cronin, S.; McCann, M.B.; Clancy, R.E.; Gore, I.; Stoudt, H.W.; Hegsted, D.M.; and Stare, F.J. "Nutritional and Epidemiologic Factors Related to Heart Disease." *World Review of Nutrition and Dietetics,* Vol. 12, 1970, pp. 1-42.

Brown, William D. "Excessive Parental Stress Guaranteed If You..." Pamphlet. Washington, DC, 1981.

_____.*Families Under Stress.* Washington, DC: Wycliff Publishing Company, 1977.

Cannon, Mark W. "Crime and the Decline of Values." Paper delivered before the Southwestern Judicial Conference, Santa Fe, New Mexico, June 4, 1981.

Caplow, Theodore. *Middletown Families.* Minneapolis: University of Minnesota Press, 1982.

Carroll, Lewis. *Alice in Wonderland.* New York: Holt, Rinehart and Winston, 1923.

Carter, Arnold. *The Amazing Results—Full World of Cassette Learning!* Chicago: The Human Resources Company, 1980.

Cherniss, Cary. "Job Burnout: Growing Worry for Workers, Bosses." *U.S. News and World Report* (February 18, 1980) 88:71ff.

Clausen, Henry C. *Clausen's Commentaries on Morals and Dogma.* Washington: The Supreme Council, 33°, Ancient and Accepted Scottish Rite of Freemasonry, 1976.

_____.*Emergence of the Mystical.* Washington: The Supreme Council, 33°, Ancient and Accepted Scottish Rite of Freemasonry, 1980.

Coles, Robert. "Our Self-Centered Children—Heirs of the 'Me' Decade." *U.S. News and World Report* (February 25, 1980) 88:80-81.

Cooper, Kenneth H. *Aerobics.* New York: Bantam Books, 1968.

Cousins, Norman. *Anatomy of an Illness.* Toronto: Bantam Books, 1979.

Culligan, Matthew J. and Sedlacek, Keith. *How to Avoid Stress Before It Kills You.* New York: Gramercy Publishing Company, 1976.

Czeisler, C.A., Richardson, G.S., Zimmerman, J.C., Moore-Ede, M.C., and Weitzman, E.D. "Entrainment of Human Circadian Rhythms by Light-dark Cycles: A Reassessment." *Photochemistry and Photobiology* (August, 1981) 34(2):239-47.

Davis, Martha; McKay, Matthew; and Eshelman, Elizabeth Robbins. *The Relaxation and Stress Reduction Workbook.* Richmond, California: New Harbinger Publications, 1980.

DeMille, Cecil B. *The Autobiography of Cecil B. DeMille.* (ed. by Donald Hayne) Englewood Cliffs, New Jersey: Prentice-Hall, Inc., 1959.

Denton, Jeremiah A. *When Hell Was in Session.* New York: Crowell Publishing Company, 1976.

De Rosis, Helen. *Women and Anxiety.* New York: Delacorte Press, 1979.

Engel vs. Vitale, June 24, 1962, 370 U.S. 421, Supreme Court.

Engel, G. "The Need for a New Medical Model: A Challenge for Biomedicine." *Science* (1977) 196:129-136.

Engeman, Thomas S. and Benson, George C.S. *Amoral America.* Stanford, California: Hoover Institution Press, 1975.

Epenshade, Thomas J. "Raising A Child Can Now Cost $85,000." *Intercom* (September, 1980) p. 1. *Famous Letters.* Westwood, New Jersey: Fleming H. Revell Company, 1968.

Finn, Chester E., Jr. "A Call for Quality Education." *Life Magazine* (March, 1981) Vol. 4, No. 3, pp. 82-98.

Flynn, Patricia Anne Randolph, *Holistic Health: the Art and Science of Care.* Bowie, Maryland: Robert J. Brady Company (A Prentice-Hall Publishing and Communications Company), 1980.

Forbes, Rosalind. *Corporate Stress: How to Manage Stress and Make It Work for You.* New York: Doubleday and Company, 1979.

_____.*Life Stress.* New York: Doubleday and Company, Inc., 1979.

Freeman, Douglas Southall. *A Register of His Papers in the Library of Congress.* Washington: Library of Congress, 1960.

Friedman, Meyer and Rosenman, Ray H. *Type A Behavior and Your Heart.* New York: Fawcett Crest, 1974.

Frye, Charles M. "Who Runs the Schools?" *Newsweek* (September 3, 1979) 94:13.

Gallup Religion Index, The. The Gallup Poll, 1981.

Glasser, William R. *Reality Therapy.* New York: Harper and Row, 1965.

Gordon, Arthur. *A Touch of Wonder.* Old Tappan, New Jersey: Fleming H. Revell Company, 1974.

Granger's Index to Poetry. "Sonnets from the Portuguese—Sonnet XLIII." New York: Columbia University Press, 1973.

Guthrie, Ann and Elliott, William A. "The Nature and Reversibility of Cerebral Impairment in Alcoholism." *Journal of Studies on Alcohol* (1980) vol. 41, no. 1, pp. 147-155.

Haro, Michael S. "T.Q. and What It Can Mean To You." Pamphlet. Houston, TX, 1981.

Haynes, S.G.; Feinleib, M.; Levine, S.; Scotch, N; and Kannel, W.B. "The Relationship of Psychosocial Factors to Coronary Heart Disease in the Framingham Study. II Prevalence of Coronary Heart Disease." *American Journal of Epidemiology* (May, 1978) 107:5:384-402.

Hegarty, Christopher J. "Do You Work too Hard? An Expert Explains the Dangers." *U.S. News and World Report* (March 26, 1979) 87:73.

Hill, Napoleon. *Think and Grow Rich.* New York: Fawcett Crest, 1957.

Hollingshead, August B. "Cultural Factors in the Selection of Marriage Mates." *American Sociological Review* (1950) 15:619-627.

Holmes, T.H. and Rahe, R.H. "The Social Readjustment Rating Scale." *Journal of Psychosomatic Research* (1967) (2)11:213-218.

Holy Bible, The (RSV). "Psalm 23." New York: Thomas Nelson and Sons, 1946.

James, William. *The Varieties of Religious Experience.* New York: Longmans Green and Company, 1935.

_____.*The Will to Believe and Other Essays in Popular Philosophy.* Cambridge: Harvard University Press, 1979.

Jarvik, M.E. (ed.) *Psychopharmacology in the Practice of Medicine.* "A Diagnosis of Affective Disorders," by Frederick K. Goodwin. New York: Appleton-Century-Crofts, 1977, pp. 219-230.

Klein, Donald F. "When Panic Strikes: Helping Anxiety Victims." *U.S. News and World Report* (June 2, 1980) 88:69ff.

Lazarus, R.S. "Little Hassles Can Be Hazardous to Health." *Psychology Today* (July, 1981) 15:48-62.

_____."Positive Denial: The Case for not Facing Reality." Interview by D. Coleman. *Psychology Today.* (November, 1979) 13:44ff.

Life Lines, No. 5, December, 1979, p. 1.

"Linkletter Interview: The Joy of Risking," *Success Magazine.* (April, 1981) p. 37ff.

List, Julie. *The Day the Loving Stopped.* Autumn, New York: Seaview Books, 1980.

Lydic, R.; Schoene, W.C.; Czeisler, C.A.; and Moore-Ede, M.C. "Suprachiasmatic Region of the Human Hypothalamus: Homolog to the Primate Circadian Pacemaker?" *Sleep,* (1980) 2(3):355-61.

Machlowitz, Marilyn. *Workaholics.* New York: Addison-Wesley Publishing Company, Inc., 1980.

Mansfield, Stephanie. "Mental Distress on the Rise." *The Washington Post,* May 23, 1980, p. A35.

Marshall, Catherine. *A Man Called Peter.* New York: McGraw-Hill 1951.

Maslow, A.H. *Motivation and Personality.* New York: Harper, 1954.

McManus and Clarke. "Life Stress Profile: A Projective Technique." Medical City, 7777 Forest Lane, #250, Dallas, Texas 75230.

McQuade, Walter. "Good News from the House on Lincoln Street: the Framingham Heart Study Is Helping the Nation Win the Long Struggle Against Coronary Heart Disease." *Fortune* (January 14, 1980) pp. 86-92.

Mead, Frank S. (ed.) *The Encyclopedia of Religious Quotations.* Westwood, New Jersey: Fleming H. Revell Company, 1960.

Mines, Herbert T. "How to Make It to the Executive Suite." *U.S. News and World Report* (August 18, 1980) 88:72ff.

Mitchell, Margaret. *Gone with the Wind.* New York: McMillan and Company, 1936.

Mitford, Jessica. *American Way of Death.* New York: Simon and Schuster, 1963.

Ornish, Dean. *Stress, Diet, & Your Heart.* New York: Holt, Rinehart and Winston, 1982.

Oursler, Fulton. *Modern Parables.* New York: Perma Books, 1952.

Patrick, Pamela. *Health Care Worker Burnout: What Is It, What to Do About It.* New York: Inquiry Books, 1980.

Pert, A. "Body's Own Tranquilizers." *Psychology Today* (September, 1981) 15:100.

Philips, Debora and Judd, Robert. *How to Fall Out of Love.* Boston: Houghton-Mifflin, Company, 1978.

Pietropinto, Anthony and Simenauer, Jacqueline. *Beyond the Male Myth.* New York: New York Times Book Company, 1978.

Robbins, Paula I. *Successful Mid-life Career Change.* New York: American Management Association, Inc., 1980.

Rosten, Leo. *The Power of Positive Nonsense.* New York: McGraw-Hill Book Company, 1977.

Royal Canadian Air Force Exercise Plans for Physical Fitness. Canada: Pocket Books, 1962.

_____.*Stress without Distress.* Philadelphia: J.P. Lippincott Company, 1974.

Schaff, Philip (ed.) *A Select Library of Nicene and Post Nicene Fathers of the Christian Church.* Buffalo: Christian Literature Company, 1887, Vol. 4.

Selye, Hans. *The Stress of Life.* New York: McGraw-Hill, 1956.

Stockdale, James B. "The World of Epictetus." *Atlantic Monthly.* (April, 1978) 241:98-106.

"Stress: A Sign of the Times." *Science News* (May 23, 1981) 119:328.

Sullivan, Harry Stack. *Clinical Studies in Psychiatry.* New York: Norton and Company, Inc., 1956.

Swanson, Lillian. "Sleep Studies Reveal Best Depression Cure." *The Free Lance-Star,* October 11, 1980, p. 23.

Thomas, Lowell. "Unforgettable Eddie Rickenbacker." *The Reader's Digest* (December 1972) pp. 109-113.

Thoreau, Henry David. *Journal.* 12 April 1852.

Tubesing, Donald A. *Kicking Your Stress Habits.* Minneapolis: Whole Person Associates, 1981.

Twelfth Annual Survey of High Achievers. Published by Who's Who Among American High School Students, 1980.

Upton Miller, Speech delivered at Honors Convocation, Ripon College, Ripon, Wisconsin, April 26, 1967.

Vickery, Donald M. *Life Plan for Your Health.* Reading, Mass: Addison-Wesley, 1978.

Wall, J.M. "Solzhenitsyn's Harvard Sermon." *Christian Century* (September 20, 1978) 95:843.

Wall Street Journal. "Employee Relocation." May 19, 1981, p. 43.

Wolfe, Thomas. *You Can't Go Home Again.* Harper and Row, 1940.

About the Author

William D. Brown, Ph.D., is a clinical psychologist in private practice in Washington, D.C., where he also writes an award-winning syndicated column on stress carried in many newspapers around the country. A widely acclaimed speaker, he travels extensively lecturing and consulting with industry on improved ways of coping with stress and establishing business ethics and integrity.

A prolific writer, Dr. Brown's publications have appeared in both professional and popular publications. He wrote "A Social-Psychological Framework of the Family," in *Emerging Conceptual Frameworks of Family Theorists* (Macmillan, 1966), edited by Nye and Berado. He is also author of *Families Under Stress* (Wycliff, 1977), which has undergone several printings.

Bill and his wife of more than twenty years, Nett, have two teen-aged children in college, Bill, Jr., and Sharon. The Browns breed Arabian horses on their place in Virginia.

Other Good Books from CompCare Publications

Do I Have To Give Up Me To Be Loved By You?, Jordan Paul, Ph.D. and Margaret Paul, Ph.D. A key book that makes all other books about relationships understandable. Intimacy *plus* personal freedom is a possible dream. The Pauls show us how to work through conflict in ways that bring intimacy.

The Hug Therapy Book, Kathleen Keating. By a mental health counselor, this book has an earnest message based on up-to-the-minute scientific knowledge: *Human touch is a basic human need.* Hugging is important for healing and health. With witty drawings of bears (who do it best!).

If Only My Wife Could Drink Like A Lady, Jack Nero. The heartening story of a 1-in-10 marriage to survive a wife's alcoholism — by her co-alcoholic husband. Ways to overcome the helpless, hopeless feelings for anyone who lives with an alcoholic.

Life Is Goodbye/Life Is Hello, Alla Bozarth-Campbell, Ph.D. A therapist and one of the first eleven women to be ordained as priests by the Episcopal church teaches a new and important skill — how to "grieve well" through all kinds of loss: death, divorce, job loss, geographic change, weight gain or loss, miscarriage, even the loss of healthy ambition that comes with success!

The Sexual Addiction, Patrick J. Carnes, Ph.D. The first book to explore the lonely, hidden world of the sexual addict — and to offer a program of hope for addicts and their families. Often handed down from one generation to the next, sexual addiction may be a family's best kept secret.

Steppin ... nthia
Lewis-S ... res a
smile-as ... nilies.
Include ... rding
progress

Surviva ... vriter,
counsel ... ntry's
best-kn ... ritual
strength ... vors"
overcom

Thin Is ... ghtful
explana ... eight.
Give u ... rough
struggle ... ge as
you liste